A
ROOM
BY
ROOM
GUIDE

SCANDINAVIAN
STYLE
at HOME

A ROOM BY ROOM GUIDE

SCANDINAVIAN STYLE at HOME

Allan Torp

Thames & Hudson

On the cover:

Front: Hammarby Allé 53b, photo Anna Malmberg, stylist Linda Palmcrantz
(www.fantasticfrank.com).

Back: Dining room, Seglatsgatan 14, photo Mikael Axelsson, stylist Emma
Wallmén (www.fantasticfrank.com); Palette JH8 table, designed by Jamie
Haylon for &Tradition.

First published in the United Kingdom in 2017 by
Thames & Hudson Ltd, 181A High Holborn, London WC1V 7QX

This book was designed and produced by
Quid Publishing, an imprint of the Quarto Group
The Old Brewery
6 Blundell Street
London N7 9BH

British Library Cataloguing-in-Publication Data
A catalogue record for this book is available from the British Library

ISBN 978-0-500-51956-1

Printed and bound in China

To find out about all our publications, please visit **www.thamesandhudson.com**.
There you can subscribe to our e-newsletter, browse or download our current
catalogue, and buy any titles that are in print.

MIX
Paper from
responsible sources
FSC® C016973

Contents

Preface

It is hard to believe today, but in the 1980s and 1990s, Scandinavian style was unfashionable. It was a time when wall-to-wall carpets and rag-rolled colourful walls prevailed. No one was interested in Scandinavian style with its wooden floors, neutral tones and simple lines. You could find once-coveted Arne Jacobsen and Hans J. Wegner furniture left on the curb, thrown out as rubbish, or pick it up for bargain prices. But that was all set to change. In the early 2000s, with a little unexpected help from world-renowned Danish restaurant Noma, the term 'new Nordic' was introduced, bringing all things Scandinavian into the limelight.

Since the dawn of the new millennium, the popularity of Scandinavian style has grown enormously, and it looks set to continue. Companies throughout Scandinavia are once again manufacturing iconic mid-20th-century designs and finding old drawings of pieces never constructed before, which are now being put into production. Some rare, original furnishings occasionally surface and sell at auction for high prices.

Scandinavian style is not only about stylish elegance, but also about functionality – your furniture needs to serve a purpose and should be long-lasting. Don't overthink your design; it should come naturally. The perfect Scandinavian-style interior will not be achieved just by painting the walls white and throwing a grey blanket on your sofa.

This book is not only about the iconic Scandinavian mid-20th-century designs, but also tells the story of how Scandinavian style developed and demonstrates how to incorporate the style into your own home.

▸ *Light, simple and calm are the key concepts that form the foundation of Scandinavian style.*

1. INTRODUCING
SCANDINAVIAN STYLE

What is Scandinavian style?

Scandinavian style is a design movement characterized by a minimalist philosophy that encourages simplicity, neutral colour schemes and functionality, which emerged in the 1940s and 1950s. The name 'Scandinavian' is in fact a little misleading, as the style developed in the five Nordic countries of Finland, Norway, Sweden, Denmark and Iceland (Scandinavia encompasses only Denmark, Sweden and Norway). The term 'Scandinavian design' arguably originates from a design show called 'Design in Scandinavia' that travelled through North America in the mid 1950s. Promoting the Scandinavian way of living, it exhibited works by Nordic designers and established the style that continues to be loved today: simple, elegant designs, inspired by nature and the northern climate, available to all, with an emphasis on creating a comfortable domestic environment.

The key principles of Scandinavian style

The founders of Scandinavian design (see pages 16–17), provided the model and set of values that endure today: durability, functionality and reliability – but also less tangible values such as equality, simplicity, comfort and pleasure, visible through the natural forms and discreet elegance.

The main purpose of Scandinavian design is to improve daily life. To accomplish that, designers focused on interior living, designing furniture, lighting, textiles, accessories and everyday utilitarian items such as dishes, silverware, cooking utensils and textiles.

In Scandinavian interiors, there is always a strong relationship between design elements and nature. It is often seen in the stark contrast between abstract and natural shapes, as well as hard and soft surfaces and materials. Natural materials such as wood, leather, wool, cotton and linen are used in most Scandinavian interiors.

◄ *Two of Danish designer Børge Mogensen's Spanish Chairs take centre stage in this stylish Scandinavian-style living room.*

The rise of Scandinavian style

Scandinavian design existed before the great mid-20th-century designers Arne Jacobsen, Børge Mogensen and Hans J. Wegner made it a globally recognized and popular design style. Its roots can be traced to the early 20th century.

Simple and traditional

At the end of the 19th century, the Nordic countries mostly consisted of poor farming areas, where only a small, wealthy upper class had any decorative items in their homes. As money was scarce, most people owned only a few simple and functional pieces of furniture. In the 1930s, a new decorative style evolved in Sweden; linked to the architectural neoclassical style, it was a combination of traditional details and simple lines, which appealed to a growing middle class. This style received some international recognition and was called Swedish Grace. This was typified by the work of Louise Adelborg (1885–1971), who, in collaboration with the manufacturer Rörstrand, designed decorative patterns and porcelain products still available today. The far more radical design movement of modernism quickly surpassed Swedish Grace.

The birth of modernism

In 1930, the Stockholm International Exhibition introduced the concept of modernism to Scandinavia. The exhibition took the Nordic countries by storm, and modernism was born. The Swedish architect Gunnar Asplund was an early convert to this new style, which was a departure from his neoclassical work of the 1920s. He wrote the functionalist manifesto *Acceptera!* (Accept!).

▲ *Launched in the 1930s, Swedish Grace, Louise Adelborg's masterful porcelain for Rörstrand, helped define a new modern style in Scandinavia.*

In the 1930s, political reforms saw the development of the welfare system, which allowed Scandinavian architects to build new hospitals, schools and housing. The domestic interiors were built along modern lines and included standardized kitchens and bathrooms, so function and hygiene were improved. Many of the young designers were influenced by the Bauhaus, which focused on creating objects that were beautiful and useful. The world also started to applaud the work coming from the Nordic countries, as Finnish architect Alvar Aalto exhibited his furniture at the

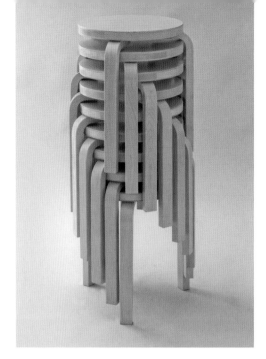

Museum of Modern Art (MoMA) in New York in 1939, while a Danish company found success with Poul Henningsen's PH pendant lamps.

Mid-20th-century heyday

In 1947, the Triennale di Milano, a popular design exhibition held in Italy, showed the work of Scandinavian designers, led by Danes Mogensen, Jacobsen, Wegner and Juhl. The success of their work, called Scandinavian Modern, quickly became famous.

Capitalizing on this newfound popularity, the 'Design in Scandinavia' show travelled throughout the US and Canada from 1954 to 1957. North Americans loved the minimalistic, functional style inspired by nature and the Nordic climate; they liked the clean, simple and elegant designs. America embraced Scandinavian style, and designers Finn Juhl, Poul Kjærholm, Kaare Klint and Alvar Aalto all became well known. They won

▲ *Alvar Aalto's simple yet functional three-legged, stackable stool is a quintessential example of functional furniture design.*

▲ *A sideboard, such as this one by Hans J. Wegner, is a useful addition to the modern dining room.*

numerous awards in international exhibitions, ensuring worldwide recognition.

Scandinavian style flourished throughout the 1950s and 1960s, led by Danish designers and a new idea from FDB (*Fællesforeningen for Danmarks Brugsforeninger*), the Danish Consumers Cooperative Society (today Coop Denmark), which wanted to produce affordable furniture for everyone. Børge Mogensen, helped by Hans J. Wegner, led the design work.

Colour makes a splash

By the end of the 1960s, the gap between industrial designers and artistic creators had closed. Slowly, an industrial, innovative and colourful style developed, but only a few Scandinavian companies benefited. Two Finnish companies – the glass manufacturer Iittala and fabric maker Marimekko – were successful, as their focus was mainly on colour. Consumers had grown tired of the neutral colour palette; they wanted colour and modern materials. One of Denmark's most influential designers, Verner Panton, found an increased interest in his distinctive, colourful plastic furniture (Vitra produces these designs).

A Scandinavian renaissance

After a decline in popularity, Scandinavian style slowly started to become fashionable again at the end of the 1980s. Swedish designers led the way, with help from Italian design companies such as Cappellini. In the UK, retailers such as Habitat and Heals sold Scandinavian products.

▶ *The work of Danish designer Verner Panton came to prominence in the 1960s when people were craving more colour.*

However, it was in the early 2000s that a true renaissance of Scandinavian style began to emerge. The term 'new Nordic' was used to describe the cooking style of Danish chefs René Redzepi and Claus Meyer with the opening of their stylish restaurant Noma, which quickly became one of the world's premier food destinations. People wanted to taste Noma's cuisine and to decorate their homes like the restaurant. This led to a renewed general interest in Scandinavian design and style.

The demand for Scandinavian style continues to grow, a reawakening of interest not only for the work of the early pioneers, but also for the many emerging new designers and architects.

The founders of Scandinavian style

The era of the 1930s to the 1970s was the golden age of Scandinavian design. A number of prominent furniture designers, known as the founders of Scandinavian philosophy and style, had a huge impact and their influence is still evident today in the work of designers worldwide. These iconic Nordic designers include Alvar Aalto, Poul Henningsen, Arne Jacobsen, Børge Mogensen, Finn Juhl, Greta Magnusson-Grossman and Hans J. Wegner.

Alvar Aalto: Alvar Aalto (1898–1976) breathed life and warmth into modernism, placing emphasis on organic geometry, natural materials and respect for the human element. Aalto's intention was to create integrated environments to be experienced through all the senses and to design furniture that would be at once modern, human and specifically Finnish. Some of his best-known work is the Aalto vase from 1936 (right) and the Bench 153A from 1945 (see pages 60–61).

Poul Henningsen: Poul Henningsen (1894–1967) achieved international recognition for his lamp designs. Because of his rather vain mother, he started designing lamps while the electrical light bulb was still considered a new technology. In 1924, he won his first award for a lamp design, which would later become the PH lamp we know today. The PH lamp and his famous Artichoke lamp (see pages 64–65) are still manufactured nearly a century later by Louis Poulsen.

▲ *Alvar Aalto's iconic vase from 1936.*

▲ *A desk lamp by Poul Henningsen, a master of lighting design.*

Arne Jacobsen: Architect Arne Jacobsen (1902–1971) was a prolific modernist designer and one of the best-known architects of his time. He designed everything from buildings to door handles, taps (see pages 150–151) and coffee pots (see pages 110–111). He was influenced by Mies van der Rohe, Le Corbusier, and Charles and Ray Eames. Some of his most famous pieces include the Ant and Egg chairs.

▲ *The Arne Jacobsen suite at the Radisson Hotel, Copenhagen.*

Børge Mogensen: Børge Mogensen (1914–1972) was dedicated to making affordable furniture for everyone. Together with the manufacturer FDB, he cemented his status as a leader of Danish design. He won many awards for his simple, yet robust and masculine designs. His best-known work is the Spanish Chair from 1958 (see page 12).

Finn Juhl: Finn Juhl (1912–1989) was one of the most influential modernist designers. He is famous for introducing Danish modern furniture to the US. Juhl worked with Niels Vodder, who constructed most of Juhl's ideas. His pieces are sculptural, elegant and characterized by his love of the arts. His best-known work is the Chieftains Chair from 1949 (right).

▲ *Perhaps Finn Juhl's best-known work, the Chieftains Chair.*

Greta Magnusson-Grossman: Greta Magnusson-Grossman (1906–1999) spent the last fifty years of her life in California, but she first established herself as a young designer in Sweden. Marrying Scandinavian and Californian modernist aesthetics, she opened a shop on Rodeo Drive in Los Angeles, selling Swedish designs to notable celebrities such as Greta Garbo and Frank Sinatra. Her best-known work is the Gräshoppa lamp (see pages 176–177).

▲ *The designs of Magnusson-Grossman were almost lost to history, but today Danish manufacturer Gubi reproduces her original designs.*

Hans J. Wegner: Hans J. Wegner (1914–2007) was a master of 20th-century Danish modernism. He was particularly fond of designing chairs, and drew more than 500, of which about 100 have been produced. Wegner's work includes iconic pieces, such as the Peacock chair, the Wishbone chair and the Shell chair (below).

There are too many influential Nordic designers to list here, but we should not forget the Danish architect Mogens Lassen (1901–1987), who designed one of the most iconic candleholders of all times, Kubus, in 1962. Jørgen Rasmussen (b. 1931) designed the Kevi chair in 1958 and the double-wheel castor, which has been used on almost every rolling office chair for the last forty years. Finally, Nanna Ditzel (1923–2005) was one of the few women in a man's world. Her designs were perhaps not as radical and groundbreaking as some of her colleagues; her most recognized piece, the Trinidad chair, was designed in 1993.

▾ *Hans J. Wegner's beautiful Shell chair was designed in 1963.*

New Scandinavian-style designers

Today, Scandinavian designs are just as sought after as they were in the 1950s. New designers are producing furniture inspired by the founders of Scandinavian style, but with their own voice and interpretation. Alliances across Nordic countries and brands are being built, and many new design companies have been set up in response to the demand for Scandinavian products.

New ideas

Some declining established brands have been forced to rethink their strategies. Fritz Hansen, Bang & Olufsen and Georg Jensen have employed well-known designers such as Ilse Crawford, Cecilie Manz and Jaime Hayon to help them to revamp their designs. Other companies such as Gubi, Skagerak and Menu turnèd to new names – GamFratesi, Norm Architects and Chris L. Halstrøm – to boost their sales with fresh ideas.

Changing colours

Many designers continue to explore and reinterpret Scandinavian style. While some look to the founding fathers, others seek inspiration outside Nordic culture. These influences introduce

▼ *The TS Table by GamFratesi is just one of many new designs making Scandinavian style popular today.*

new materials and colours. Scandinavian style is still characterized by simplicity and functionality; however, the neutral colour palette is changing with input from the fashion world and beyond. Now, a sofa in a neutral grey tone might be paired with a set of armchairs in muted green, or styled with colourful cushions.

Continuing the legacy

Since the mid 2000s, many new brands have emerged. Some started out with only a few original designs, but because of the huge global interest in Scandinavian style, they have developed into successful businesses. A number of owners have sold their companies for small fortunes, while others continue to work. However, what matters to designers is continuing the legacy of the founding fathers who laid the foundations for Scandinavian style in the 20th century.

▲ Danish company Skagerak was transformed from an old-fashioned brand into something new and modern, with the help of young designer Chris L. Halstrøm, who designed this bench.

▶ Finnish firm Marimekko has for decades designed unique colourful patterns to fit the Scandinavian style.

IKEA

Some may immediately think of the primary blue and yellow buildings of IKEA as the main source of Scandinavian design, but there is so much more to Scandinavian style than this iconic store. IKEA has, however, increased its accessibility worldwide. Their catalogue, which has the world's largest print production, is full of ideas and is a great inspiration if you are new to Scandinavian style.

Bringing Scandinavian style to the world
It all started with a strong concept by 17-year-old Ingvar Kamprad, who started a mail-order business from his childhood home. The idea was to sell self-assembled furniture, and his first small tables are still in production today.

While many may consider IKEA to be a place where you buy everything for your first apartment, and then upgrade, it has in fact been a hugely influential player in bringing Scandinavian style to every corner of the world. IKEA has been a

pioneer in sustainable and mass production, and has created many iconic pieces. In the past, it relied on its own in-house designers but, in recent times, international figures such as Ilse Crawford and Tom Dixon have created dynamic collections for the company.

Accessible for all
From the start, IKEA merged trends from both the interior design and fashion worlds, making low-cost products for everyone. It has played a major part in developing Scandinavian design, making it accessible for all, just like the philosophy of the founding fathers. By selling small household items as well as chairs, tables, sofas, beds and soft furnishings, it allows consumers to furnish their homes in a functional and affordable way. IKEA has become so ubiquitous worldwide that it is possible to suggest every person will, at some point in their life, own something from IKEA.

◄ *Ilse Crawford's collection for IKEA, which made use of natural materials such as cork, ceramics and glass, sold out in just a few weeks when it first went on the market in October 2015; only a few pieces are still in production.*

2. ACHIEVING THE LOOK

Form and functionality

Scandinavian style is characterized by form, functionality, simplicity and clean lines. According to its design principles, one should be in harmony with one's environment, and objects should be made to last rather than be replaced. To complement the art of living well, the design philosophy promotes a simple home environment and an unencumbered, uncluttered lifestyle.

Easy living

Scandinavian style is all about having a flow that allows easy living in an open and airy setting. At the end of the 1990s, Scandinavians opted for open-plan living to encompass the kitchen, dining room and lounge. Knocking down walls between the rooms made even the smallest homes appear larger and brighter. Fresh, white kitchens included islands to make the kitchen an even bigger part of the dining and living space.

Opening up the living space also encourages clutter-free living, as you are more likely to maintain a tidy space when everything is on view. Opt for built-in furniture to create a streamlined look and dispose of unnecessary clutter. Only display those items that are modern and stylish. Store everything else to achieve a calm, stress-free atmosphere.

Art also helps to achieve a serene home. Culture and art play a large role in Scandinavian life, so it is only natural for this to show up in their interiors. The choice of art can be left to your taste; there is no right or wrong. It can be as colourful and provocative as you want it to be. Even the most colourful painting can complement the most neutral-coloured Scandinavian interior.

Key design pieces

The main purpose of Scandinavian design is to improve daily life. To accomplish this, designers focused on interior design style with furniture, lighting, textiles, accessories and everyday utilitarian items like dishes, silverware, cooking utensils and linen.

To achieve true Scandinavian style, it is important to have at least one piece created or influenced by one of the designers mentioned on pages 16–18. Remember that one of the key points in Scandinavian style is functionality: it is not only about looking good; your furniture needs to have function and should also be long-lasting. Look at the Key Pieces in Section 3 for inspiration on how iconic items can provide a focal point or mood for a room.

▲ *Originally designed in 1958 by Arne Jacobsen, the Egg chair might be one of the most recognizable chairs in modern design.*

◄ *The space in this huge room has been broken up by inserting a partition wall, creating an en-suite bathroom.*

Natural materials

In Scandinavian interiors, there is a strong relationship between design elements and nature. The Nordic countries have many forests, and wood especially has played a key role in interiors. The richness of wooden boards or a perfectly handcrafted wooden chair speaks to Scandinavians. Bringing natural materials inside helps them to feel surrounded by nature. It's often seen in the stark contrast between abstract and natural shapes, as well as hard and soft surfaces and materials. Natural materials like stone, wood, leather and linen are used thoughtfully in most home interiors. Scandinavian design seamlessly

▲ *In recent years, green plants have made a huge comeback in Scandinavian interior design.*

▶ *A hint of green from plants or accessories is a great addition to a classic all-white Scandinavian-style dining room.*

blends various materials. Against a neutral backdrop, leather, wool, metal, concrete and wood can live harmoniously together. The critical component is to keep the tones of the materials within a similar colour range, for example, white and grey. Otherwise, the use of varied materials will clutter the space and make it feel fussy, which is the opposite of what the design scheme is attempting to achieve.

▲ Keeping your overall colour scheme neutral, for example, using whites and greys, will allow your carefully selected natural items to shine through, as seen here in this space.

A love of nature

Scandinavians have a deep-rooted love of nature. Hobbies revolve around outdoor activities such as biking, hiking and skiing – they take every opportunity to enjoy the great outdoors.

During the long, cold winter, it is easy to forget the natural beauty and warmth of summer, so bring nature inside to beat the winter blues. Add woollen throws to a wooden armchair and light an open fire or wood burner to create the natural feel of Scandinavian style.

Houseplants have made a big comeback. Green plants were a major part of Scandinavian interior design in the 1970s and 1980s, but during the minimalistic phase of the 1990s and 2000s, they became less common. However, displaying houseplants is one of the easiest ways to introduce nature into the home.

Neutral colours

Pure, simple and restful colours have become the trademark of Scandinavian design and seem to be one of the main draws to its global popularity. Think white, beige and grey, and pale and dusky tones. These colours are unique to Scandinavian minimalism – especially the combination of grey and beige, which is not often seen elsewhere in minimalist designs. However, it is becoming increasingly common to inject splashes of colour to add interest to a decor scheme. Regardless of colour choices, it is the design aesthetic – simple, streamlined and unfussy – that translates to a true Scandinavian interior.

The backdrop

A good starting point is a neutral backdrop and the easiest way to achieve this is with stark white walls. This clean, blank canvas is timeless. White walls are perfect, even when you decide to change the look of the room or its accessories. To add contrast, spaces can be brightened up with bold tones and accent colours in the accessories or furnishings.

▼ Neutral tones dominate in the Scandinavian style, but these can be broken up with additions in bold colours, as seen in this open-plan room, where blacks and dark grey accessories have been used.

◀ *The Mayor sofa designed by Arne Jacobsen in 1939, as seen here, was created for Søllerød City Hall, and is still manufactured today to its original design.*

▼ *Colourful cushions with bold prints are an easy way to add a splash of colour to any Scandinavian-style room.*

A splash of colour

Not all Scandinavian designs are muted and calm. Some noteworthy designers prefer a much bolder design statement, such as the popular Marimekko, a Finnish design company that produces colourful graphic designs.

Some new Danish brands are pushing the boundaries of what is considered a traditional Scandinavian colour palette. They are playing with different colours not normally seen in Scandinavian design, by introducing a richer and warmer selection of colours, such as blue, mustard and red – proving that it is possible to decorate with bold and colourful furniture and still be true to Scandinavian style. As people travel more, it is no surprise that trends from around the world have influenced Scandinavian style, but the muted and calm colour palette remains. Colours might slowly be moving into Scandinavian interiors, but it is important not to go overboard or try to colour-coordinate a room: a few accent colours will achieve the look.

Prints and patterns

Whether you prefer bright, bold interiors or a calm and serene quality, you can certainly achieve a distinctly Scandinavian style in your modern home.

Don't get carried away when choosing colours and prints; just one wall with a beautiful hand-painted wallpaper, or a cushion with a fun, patterned print on a grey couch, works well. Recognized patterns also work, such as the iconic blue-and-white chequered Hästens bed (see pages 178–179), Marimekko's classic poppy print Unikko or the colourful patterns in one of the many throws from Norwegian Røros Tweed.

Brands worldwide have seen the potential of the Scandinavian colour palette, and some companies have even become popular among Scandinavians, such as British colour specialists Farrow & Ball, whose products have distinctly Scandinavian tones.

Simple, yet cosy

▲ *To create your own* hygge *space, it really doesn't take more than making a reading corner with a vintage lounge leather chair and a knitted blanket; anything to keep you warm and cosy.*

It is impossible to talk about Scandinavian style without mentioning *hygge*. Originally a Norwegian word meaning 'well-being', *hygge* first appeared in Danish writing in the 18th century. There is no perfect translation, but it roughly translates as cosiness. Today, each Nordic country claims its own specific word to describe *hygge*; in Denmark, they call it *hyggelig*; in Sweden, they call it *mysig* (pronounced myh-seeg); and in Norway they call it *koselig* (pronounced cosh-a-lee). They all relate to the same ability of finding intimacy, conviviality and cosiness in life's everyday moments. The art of *hygge* is as much about atmosphere as it is about companionship, as essential to the culture of Scandinavia as pork roast and Aquavit.

The harsh Nordic climate and long, dark winters have created the need for its inhabitants to fully enjoy those everyday moments by turning their homes into havens. A welcoming sanctuary for connecting with loved ones, but also a cocoon providing calm and stillness after a busy day; a comfortable, personal, laid-back space with natural materials and clean lines. In other words, a home filled with the spirit of *hygge*.

That certain something

Hygge has been part of Scandinavian life for centuries, and while non-Scandinavian writers may struggle to understand its true meaning, it is in fact just something that comes naturally to most Scandinavians. If you try too hard, it becomes forced. The trick is to do whatever comes naturally to you. There is no right or wrong to *hygge*. It is very real and alive, albeit difficult to explain. Certainly there are things that help, but *hygge* is everything and everywhere. *Hygge* is a cup of coffee, reading a book in a comfortable chair or being with a friend at the local coffee shop, just as much as it's a group of friends around a candlelit dining table laden with food.

▶ *A sheepskin draped over a chair adds Scandinavian-style* hygge *to the dining room.*

▼ *This cosy Scandinavian-style living room is styled simply in grey, with cushions in dusty red added for warmth and comfort; a touch of* hygge.

Floor-to-ceiling wood

▲ *Rugs add a splash of colour to hardwood floors in a room. They can also help to break up the space in an open-plan room, giving the impression of multiple rooms in one.*

Scandinavian style uses hardwood for floors and wall panelling. Often the wood is used floor to ceiling, which helps to give the impression of a larger space, by bringing in more light. Variations on this style use pale-coloured wood such as pine or birch that help to reflect light, to give rooms a spacious feel.

Hardwood floors

Unlike British or North American homes, fitted carpets are rarely used in Scandinavian interiors. Traditionally, flooring is hardwood and either painted white or left in its natural colour. This elevates the luminosity and plays off similar tones in the walls and furniture, giving a sense of light and space that helps people to live through the long, dark Scandinavian winters.

It is easy to understand why hardwood flooring is so popular when one looks at rooms designed in this way. Hardwood floors make rooms seem open, airy and clean. They draw attention to the interior quality of a room's architecture and furnishings.

The Danish company Dinesen has produced beautiful wood floors for over one hundred years. They use different types of wood, from wide oak planks to Douglas fir.

The occasional rug

While Scandinavians prefer hardwood floors, rugs – more specifically area rugs, especially under the dining table or in the living room – are often used to create warmth and *hygge* – even a rug can be considered *hygge*! They can add a splash of colour and texture to a room. How much colour or how much Middle Eastern style you want to incorporate is up to you; there are no golden rules. Handmade rugs can easily be incorporated into Scandinavian style. Choose a pattern that is not too confusing for the eye, in a calm colour scheme, with a splash of an accent colour. Wool and cotton are the go-to materials, while the thread length of the actual rug is up to the owner's taste – as long as you stick with a calmer colour scheme, you are safely within the bounds of Scandinavian style.

▼ *The use of a traditional Middle Eastern rug has been popular for adding colour and can easily be incorporated into the Scandinavian style.*

Let there be light

Natural light is of the utmost importance to Scandinavian style: flood your home with as much of it as you can, and for as long in the day as possible. With upwards of four months of short days during Scandinavian winters, light can become revered. This is what most Scandinavians deal with every winter, depending on their location: the further north, the shorter the days. Cosiness is not just candlelight on dark evenings, but bright days filled with warmth and comfort.

▲ *Norwegian blogger Elisabeth Heier makes the most of natural light; and for those long Scandinavian winter nights, the Semi pendant lamp, made by Gubi, is functional and stylish.*

Windows

Keeping window decoration to a minimum reflects the sentiment of inviting in as much light as possible. In Scandinavian-style homes, it is rare to have coverings over the windows. If there were a need to have something to cover the window, it would be preferable to use light fabrics such as linen and sheers. Often, though, these are purely for decoration and privacy rather than for functional reasons.

Multiple light sources

In Scandinavia, it is rare to have a single light source in any room, such as overhead spotlights. Instead, you are likely to find well-thought-out pendant lights, combined with floor and table lamps. Spotlights, if used at all, are on dimmer switches. And any one or combination of these, together with candles, may be used to create *hygge*.

Pendant lights

As kings of design, Scandinavians have mastered creating interesting pendant lights. This is as evident in the most affordable IKEA varieties as it is in the high-range designs; from the mid-century favourite Artichoke lamp by Poul Henningsen for Louis Poulsen (see pages 64–65) to the modern pendant Caravaggio light designed by Cecilie Manz (right).

Candles

Scandinavians use more candles per capita than any other population on earth. Perhaps it's the endless winter darkness that forces them to create

beauty in the dark. Candles are essential to a true *hygge* atmosphere. Walk down a street in Copenhagen or Stockholm on a winter evening, and you will notice every bar and café awash with candlelight. Popular throughout the world, scented-candle companies like Swedish Byredo or Danish Skandinavisk are paying tribute to the Scandinavian language not only by honouring simple words as names for the different candles, such as *skog* (forest), but also by making the scents reminiscent of the Norwegian fjords or Swedish fir forests.

▲ *Even if you are lucky enough to have a great source of natural light in your room, you still need lamps to create the right ambience.*

▶ *The Caravaggio pendant light designed by Cecilie Manz for Danish company Lightyears was launched in 2005 and has since become a contemporary icon in lighting design.*

Scandinavian furniture

While modern Scandinavian furniture takes advantage of innovative materials and techniques, such as converting recycled plastic bottles into lamps, the earlier pioneers took a more traditional approach to design and manufacturing. Amazing craftsmanship can still be seen in today's Scandinavian homes, incorporating great new designs alongside mid-century pieces.

Simplistic, yet artful

No matter what decade it's made in, attention to detail and high-quality materials will always feature in Scandinavian furniture designs. A simplistic yet artful approach reveals itself through the use of simple straight lines combined with understated embellishments.

Each piece is like an art object and will last a lifetime. This is the reason that there are many early pieces still on the market. If an original mid-century piece is out of your price range, then look at contemporary furniture designers who are making an impact.

Nature's touch

Nature's own materials, such as wood and leather, play a big part in Scandinavian style. As we have

▶ *The Series 7™ chair by Arne Jacobsen is one of the designer's most popular models and manufacturer Fritz Hansen's most regularly sold dining chair.*

already established, wooden floors and furniture predominate. The founding fathers combined these materials with leather, which has become a favoured combination for interior design. A larger wooden dining table surrounded by Arne Jacobsen's Series 7™ chairs (below left) is a common sight in many Nordic homes.

Timeless design

For more than half a century, Scandinavian design has become famous for being simple, practical, streamlined, functional and, perhaps most importantly, comfortable. You only need to look at Danish designer Hans Wegner's Wishbone chair (right) to understand how smart design can transcend time and trends. First introduced in 1949, the Wishbone chair has been extremely successful in Scandinavian decor. It is as cool today as it was over sixty-five years ago and works well in all interiors, not just traditional Scandinavian homes.

▲ *Hans J. Wegner's Wishbone chair, seen here in this dining room, has been in continuous production by Danish company Carl Hansen & Son since its launch in 1949.*

◄ *Danish company Gubi have, in recent years, reproduced many of Swedish designer Greta Magnusson-Grossman's timeless mid-century pieces.*

Ceramics and glass

Bearing in mind the Scandinavian aesthetic of functionality, simplicity and neutral colour schemes, the design of glassware and ceramics follows the same trend. The whole idea of glass art is relatively new in Scandinavia, and it wasn't until the 1920s, when Swedish company Orrefors started producing glass vases, that the material came to life in the Scandinavian style. With ceramics it was a little bit different. The inventive glazes, colours and designs made modern Scandinavian ceramics leaders, with very few international competitors.

Handmade

Handmade products became popular in the 1950s and have been an important element of Scandinavian style, not only in furniture making, but also in creating glass and ceramic objects. Swedish companies Orrefors and Kosta Boda were market leaders of glass production for many years, but as people demanded more colourful glass art, Finnish littala secured its spot in the limelight. Finnish glass is very different from Swedish – less direct and flirtatious, but just as advanced and refined. One of the best-known mid-century glass vases is arguably the Aalto vase from the 1930s, while one of today's best-known pieces is the Dagg vase from 2009 by Carina Seth Andersson for Swedish Svenskt Tenn (see pages 62–63).

Ceramic production was led by Finnish Arabia and Swedish

◄ *Danish Kähler's Omaggio vase is seen in many Scandinavian-style homes. The version pictured here has silver stripes.*

Rörstrand, both no longer in business today, but throughout Scandinavia you would find a lot of smaller independent workshops led by designers like Axel Salto and Grethe Meyer. Throughout the 1970s, 1980s and 1990s interest in ceramics dwindled, but since 2000, there has been a growing market for independent, handmade products. Danish company Kähler, which has produced ceramics for several generations, has seen a huge interest in their modern ceramics, in particular their colourful striped vases.

▲ *Gathering up your ceramic collection, however varied the sizes and colours, and displaying them together can make for an eye-catching feature.*

Old and new

Glass is great for vases, and often seen with or without flowers, as decoration only. Try to mix it in with your ceramics, both new and vintage. Scandinavian style, especially when it comes to the accessories, is a bit more open to showing your own personality. Mixing new with old is perfect, and even better if some of your collection has a story to tell: perhaps something passed to you by your grandmother, or an item you found in a flea market on holiday.

Metals

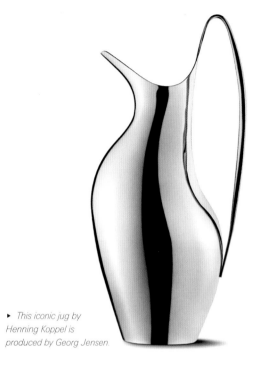

▶ *This iconic jug by Henning Koppel is produced by Georg Jensen.*

Coffee pots and cutlery

Among Scandinavians, one of the most recognized coffee pots is Arne Jacobsen's 1967 Cylinda Line designed for Danish company Stelton. The Cylinda Line collection is a good example of how Arne Jacobsen was influenced by the Bauhaus movement. Stelton followed this success with another coffee pot designed by Erik Magnussen in 1977, the EM77, which was made not from metal, but from plastic.

In Scandinavian style, the item most obviously made from steel is cutlery. Norwegian Tias Eckhoff designed the popular Maya series, which was a huge success in the 1950s. Arne Jacobsen also created several cutlery sets, today available from Georg Jensen. In 1938, Kay Bojesen, who is mostly known for playful wooden animals, created his set 'Grand Prix', still in production today.

Metal has been used for decoration in Scandinavia since the Viking age. The Danish company Georg Jensen is one of the world's best-known producers of metal and silver decorations. In the early days of Georg Jensen (pre 1920s), it was famous for its work in silver. In the 1950s, there was a revival of interest in its products, some of which were designed by Henning Koppel and Nanna Ditzel. Today, some of the most iconic pieces are by Koppel, such as the fish dish in silver, which takes up to six months to produce. More within reach of most people is his iconic pitcher in polished steel – a true work of art. Since the 1950s, silver has slowly been overtaken by stainless steel as the preferred metal used in Scandinavian-style designs.

▲ *This mid-century modern stainless-steel Cylinda Line tea set was designed by Arne Jacobsen for Stelton.*

Brass and copper

At the beginning of the 21st century, brass and copper started to appear in Scandinavian-style designs. And just a decade later, you can find brass and copper details on everything from lamps above the dining table and candleholders in the living room, to taps in the bathroom and knobs in the kitchen. For a while, almost every item you found in stainless steel would also have brass and copper

▲ *A copper version of Mogens Lassen's iconic Kubus candleholder.*

versions. For example, Mogens Lassen's 1962 candleholder (see pages 134–135) was originally only produced in black lacquered steel, but from 2008 it was also manufactured from brass, copper and nickel.

3. A ROOM-BY-ROOM GUIDE

ENTERING

The entryway

An entryway creates the first impression of your home. It is from here that you greet guests, so it is important that it is well decorated and carefully furnished. Whether you have a grand foyer or a simple lobby, the design should reflect your home's overall style and personality. Consider functionality as well as aesthetics to achieve a Scandinavian look that creates a stylish and organized entry space.

▲ If space is an issue in your entryway, keep it simple with just the necessities; chairs are a very useful addition.

▶ Create a clutter-free zone in your entryway with the use of a storage unit; this one doubles up as a bench, which makes it easier to put shoes on and take them off upon entering or leaving the house.

Clutter-free zone

Like all other rooms in the Scandinavian-style home, a clutter-free zone is essential. Nothing is less welcoming than an entryway full of shoes, jackets and bags.

Front entries often become a drop zone for stuff. Instead of letting the clutter win, embrace it by adding entryway storage for keys, bags, coats and shoes. Organize the space by giving each item a designated area; this will help people to focus on the decor. If lots of people live in your home, give everyone a drop spot and include a little extra space for guests.

When designing your ideal space, imagine leaving and entering your home as a guest. What do you first see: a pile of shoes or winter and summer jackets? What impression do you wish to give? Use what you have observed to make your ideal entryway.

Decorating

To turn a bland area into a stylish space, combine different colours, textures and materials, such as metal and wood.Choose decor and furniture that are light and tough at the same time. Use pale colours on the walls, as dark colours can make a cramped space appear even smaller. Don't fill your entry with dark, heavy wooden furniture. Many Scandinavian brands, such as IKEA and Montana, have great light and practical solutions.

▸ *The hallway is a great place to show off your personality with a carefully selected picture wall.*

▾ *This bench by Swedish designer Afteroom is a tribute to the Bauhaus. The connected bench and table is a simple but perfect piece of furniture for the hallway.*

Have fun with your entryway design: hooks, bowls and trays don't have to be boring! Whether you like old school, new and modern, or a combination, you can still achieve the Scandinavian look. The furniture company TON, known for its bentwood technique chairs, is also popular in Scandinavian-style homes. TON's coat hanger fits well in the Scandinavian-style entry; mix it with a modern mirror by Tati Mirror designed by Mats Broberg and Johan Ridderstråle for Swedish Asplund, and the Afteroom bench from Danish Menu.

If you have open wall space, hang artwork or photographs. The most successful hallway ideas incorporate personalized touches as well as functional pieces. Additionally, if you have a large space, fresh flowers and carefully considered ornaments placed on a table or shelf create an interesting and elegant interior.

Colours

There are no hard-and-fast rules about the use of colour in a Scandinavian-style entryway. It depends on how much natural light is available. If your entry has no or a very limited amount of natural light, it is important to keep the walls as bright as possible: white to a very light grey works well, though you could go darker if your entrance hall has a big window. Some Scandinavian-style entryways use soft blue and grey tones, where both panels and doors are painted the same colour, which gives a regal and grand look, particularly in Scandinavian homes with high ceilings and original panelling.

Case study

Owner Lotta Agaton > **Year(s)** 2016 > **Place** Stockholm, Sweden

The muted balanced colours of this entryway, with just the right amount of warmer earthy tones, is the perfect example of how to welcome Scandinavian style into the entryway. You will want as much light in the space as possible, so the temptation is to go with all-white walls. However, a clever colour-blocking paint job, like the one shown in this example, with panels in the same grey tone but with an all-white ceiling, brings back the openness and a feeling of a high ceiling in a narrow entry. Finally, adding personality helps. As shown in the example, prints, quirky vintage finds, plants and a cool mirror will do the trick. If you have chosen a darker colour on the walls, think about adding brighter elements, like the all-white moon lamp, the fun quote on a noticeboard and the light wooden chair.

Plants *Some plants can easily survive with almost no light – choose wisely though.*

Colour *This is a perfect example of how to do colour blocking with a darker colour. However, if not done right, darker walls in an entryway can go terribly wrong. If in doubt, go for an all-white floor-to-ceiling look.*

Seating *Choose a chair or bench that also works as a piece of art. A chair that is too basic will look out of place.*

Prints *Personally curated pictures and prints add personality and create a welcoming atmosphere.*

Lighting *There are many modern and mid-century lighting choices, depending on your preferred style. A bigger statement lamp needs a big personality to pull off, but in the right setting it works.*

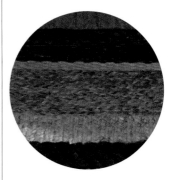

Rug *A Scandinavian-style rug in the right muted, coordinated colour scheme shows that you have mastered the style to perfection.*

Signature colours

The entryway gives the first impression of your home and is the best place to start when redecorating.

It's important to create a flow between spaces, so ensure you choose a colour that complements the colours used in rooms coming off the hallway. It can work well to choose a tone that is darker than that used in the adjacent rooms, as this will make them seem lighter and more airy by comparison. However, be careful not to go too dark. A good approach is to paint just one or two of the walls a darker colour, such as a blue or grey shade, while keeping the rest of the walls, ceiling and doors white. This is a clever way to make a long, narrow hallway feel more spacious – it will help to prevent a tunnel-like effect.

If you are lucky enough to have original wooden floors, keep them; if not, opt for a darker tile. It is easier to maintain and is a perfect contrast to the white walls.

Adding furniture should be the final thing you do. Find pieces that tell something about you and your style in the rest of your home. A vintage brown leather piece, set against a dark wall, adds a distinctive flair that will demonstrate just how well you understand Scandinavian style.

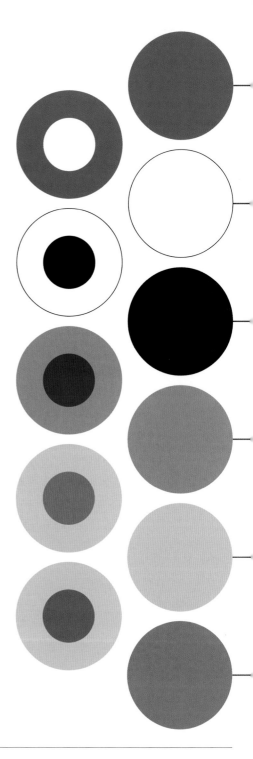

Planet Lamp

Mette Schelde (b. 1985) quickly made a name for herself after graduating from The School of Architecture in Copenhagen, Denmark, in 2013. She likes to encourage interaction between objects and the space in which they exist, which is reflected in her furniture and architectural designs.

Schelde's conceptual approach combines experimental and playful functions using materials such as wood, stone and steel. The circular discs, available in a variety of colours, are attached by magnets and can be moved around, allowing you to adapt the light for different spaces. The halogen light emits an indirect ambient glow, and creates an assortment of shadows depending on how the discs are configured.

Designer
Mette Schelde

Manufacturer
Please Wait To Be Seated

Year
2014

Place
Denmark

Material(s)
Powder-coated steel, aluminium and solid brass

Dimensions
Length: 98 cm
Depth: 12 cm

Montana Hall Edition

Montana is a modular shelving system designed for the entryway. It consists of storage boxes, a bench, mirror, racks and rails that can all be combined freely to suit any space.

The man behind the Montana Hall Edition is Peter Lassen (b. 1930), who founded the company in 1982. The system is inspired by the quadratic bookcases designed by Danish architect Mogens Koch in 1928, which are reknowned for their simplicity and flexibility of use. Taking this simple idea, Lassen has developed a storage system that is more than just a single square unit. Its design offers seemingly endless storage possibilties, making it adaptable and useful not only for the entryway, but any room where storage is needed.

Designer
Peter Lassen

Manufacturer
Montana

Year
1982

Place
Denmark

Material(s)
12 mm-thick MDF, available in forty-two water-based lacquer colours

Dimensions
Various

153A bench

As an eloquent humanist, as well as one of the great architects and designers of the 20th century, Alvar Aalto breathed life and warmth into modernism, placing emphasis on organic geometry, supple, natural materials and respect for the human element. 'Architecture', he said, 'must have charm; it is a factor of beauty in society. But real beauty is not a conception of form. it is the result of harmony between several intrinsic factors, not the least, the social.' Aalto's intention was to create integrated environments to be experienced through all the senses and to design furniture that would be at once modern, human and specifically Finnish.

For more than eighty years, Finnish Artek has shaped Scandinavian design aesthetics. It was founded in December 1935 by Alvar and Aino Aalto, Maire Gullichsen and Nils-Gustav Hahl. The founders chose a non-Finnish name, the neologism Artek, meant to manifest the desire to combine art and technology. Aalto's revolutionary ability and methods for bending wood to achieve the organic sculptural shapes of his designs made his work icons of today.

Alvar Aalto designed Artek's 153A and 153B (a smaller version of 153A) benches in 1945, but they continue to charm with their simple elegance. The airy seat is made of solid birch and rests on Aalto's signature design, the L-legs. The stylish benches are a great addition to any hallway, in the bedroom as a side table or in the living room as a coffee table.

Designer
Alvar Aalto

Manufacturer
Artek

Year
1945

Place
Finland

Material(s)
Birch

Dimensions
Height: 44 cm
Width: 112.5 cm
Depth: 40 cm

Dagg vase

An entryway is a place to create a good first impression and accessories are a great way to achieve this. This Dagg vase is one of a series of glassworks that Swedish artist and designer Carina Seth Andersson was commissioned by Svenskt Tenn to create in 2009. These pieces are intended to reflect the values of the company, which was founded by Estrid Ericson. They are inspired by the objects that Ericson had brought home as souvenirs from her travels in Scandinavia. Seth Andersson used these to contemplate how the exotic lies in nature.

Three vases were developed – Dagg, Stubbe and Kotte. Each piece varies in form, surface pattern and size, and is unique in evoking the natural environment of Sweden. Dagg draws inspiration from early misty mornings, where small drops of water hang from leaves and branches, is blown in a graphite mould at Skruf Glassworks in Småland, Sweden. The specific form of the vase requires enormous precision from the glassblower. Occasional bubbles can occur in the glass. This is a sign of real craftsmanship and should be seen as a friendly greeting from the glassblower to you.

Designer
Carina Seth Andersson

Manufacturer
Svenskt Tenn

Year
2009

Place
Sweden

Material(s)
Glass

Dimensions
Height: 27 cm
Diameter: 27 cm

PH Artichoke lamp

The Artichoke lamp is one of the most
extravagant-looking modernist lamps, suited for
larger entryways with high ceilings. The original
version of this 72-leaf lamp is made in copper with
a light rose-coloured interior. Danish lighting
manufacturer Louis Poulsen produced the first PH
lamps, and today it also manufactures a stainless-
steel version.

The designer, Poul Henningsen, is among the
best-known architects in Denmark; so much so, he
is referred to just as 'PH'. Henningsen and Louis
Poulsen have had a close working relationship
since the beginning of PH's career in 1924. After
the Second World War, PH continued to design
lamps for Louis Poulsen, including the large
Artichoke lamp, which was developed for
Langelinie Pavillonen – a restaurant in Copenhagen,
not far from the Little Mermaid – in 1957.

The lamp is one hundred per cent glare-free,
which became one of the trademark features of
PH's designs. Each leaf on the lamp is cut by laser,
for precision, and assembled by hand.

Designer
Poul Henningsen

Manufacturer
Louis Poulsen

Year
1957

Place
Denmark

Material(s)
Copper or stainless-steel frame;
laser-cut punched copper or steel
leaves

Dimensions
Height: 49.7 cm
Diameter: 48 cm

RELAXING

The living room

A Scandinavian-style living room can serve many different functions, from a formal seating area to a casual living space. The space should make your family and guests feel comfortable, but also be functional for day-to-day living. Think about the main purpose of the space and focus on a few essential items first, such as a comfortable sofa and a coffee table. Then you can choose the rest of the furniture and decor to complement the primary pieces.

Living rooms were originally intended to act as a sophisticated setting for hosting and entertaining, while family rooms were used for more casual, everyday activities, such as lounging, playing or watching TV. However, today many Scandinavian homes only have one large room that acts as both an entertainment and main living space. If yours is the former, you might be utilizing it as a formal drawing room to have drinks and entertain guests, without distractions like TV. A bar trolley, formal furniture and an eye-catching focal point, such as a sophisticated fireplace and mantel, would all help to achieve the look and feel of a Scandinavian living room.

However, if the living room is your primary living space, it will see daily use, possibly functioning as a TV room, with a sofa, media console and gaming spot. In the end, think about your needs when considering different living-room ideas; after all, a family with small children will probably need a playroom more than a formal sitting room.

▲ *Rather than one big table, group together two smaller ones for more flexibility in your living room.*

▶ *Often just a simple touch, like adding a small branch to a vase, can be enough to add a tasteful, natural element to your living room.*

Seating

You will need some seating options incorporated into your Scandinavian living-room design, which can range from easy chairs to a big, roomy sofa. Be careful of cramming a large sofa into a small

space; it's tempting to go big, but sacrificing walking paths or potential storage space is not ideal. The size of the room should determine how big your sofa should be. Even if you have a large living room, it doesn't mean that you should choose a huge sofa; you might want to add two armchairs, or maybe have two smaller couches. If you have a small room, opt for a small sofa.

Whatever design you choose, it should complement the space and not overwhelm it.

You need to have enough seating for those living at home, plus an extra seat or two for guests. An accent chair is a good way to elevate a space without making a huge investment; it may also function as an extra seat around the dining table. Whether it is a vintage leather club chair or a sleek and slender mid-century dining chair, choose something that will make a statement. Good options can be found at Sweden's oldest furniture manufacturer, Front, or the Danish furniture company, Carl Hansen and Søn, which manufactures some of the most iconic mid-century furniture. If the room allows it, a signature lounge chair could be incorporated; the Pelican Chair by Finn Juhl, in grey wool, is as much a piece of sculpture as a piece of furniture.

Television

This is definitely not an easy subject; the TV can be the elephant in the room. Decorating around the shiny black rectangle that every decade seems to grow larger can be a tricky business. Luckily, TVs have also become slimmer. In Scandinavian-style living rooms, the TV is nowadays a slim version that can be hung neatly on the wall.

Storage

If your home is generally tight on space, having plenty of shelves, cabinets or drawers will be crucial to accommodating any storage needs. Built-in cupboards are a good way to do this, since they take up less space and are often customized to meet your needs, but they can be expensive.

If built-in storage is not an option, start with the big pieces, like an entertainment centre or TV stand to house any electronics and accessories, or a bookcase to keep books, display pictures and knick-knacks. Balance is key: if you have a heavy

▼ *In this living room, the neutral, white colours have been broken up with the inclusion of natural elements like wood and green plants. Sheepskins also add texture. The wall-mounted TV is unobtrusive.*

piece with elaborate fronts to conceal your TV, you should opt for an open, more airy, storage solution for your books. Many of the Scandinavian brands have good expandable modular systems that never wear out, some in powder-coated metal, some in wood, and some combining the two; for example Ferm Living's Punctual, Menu's Stick System or the String® system (see pages 86–87).

Colour

When thinking about Scandinavian living-room colours, most people have a tendency to go super neutral or boldly colourful, but be careful of going overboard with either. If you choose neutral colours for the big items, like sofas, armchairs and ottomans, then go a bit bold with decorative accessories – that way, you can easily swap the small things when a new colour scheme is desired. Likewise, if you want your sofa to be a statement piece, scale back the decor so it does not detract attention from the furnishing.

▲ *The Wing chair by Hans J. Wegner is beautiful and simple, but also very comfortable.*

Light

Lighting is also an important feature to consider when decorating a Scandinavian living room. Can you have overhead lighting, or will you need to use table and floor lamps? Either one can be a design feature, as well as putting the spotlight on other decor you want to display. Position lighting to illuminate any art you may have, and remember to have a well-lit spot for reading. You can also change the light of the space by the paint colour you choose; a room with little natural light will benefit from a light and airy colour, such as muted greys or very pale earthy tones, while one with plenty of sunlight may allow for more colour choices, meaning that you can be bolder in your choice of colour on accessories, because you want to keep the walls quite neutral.

◄ *Finn Juhl's Pelican Chair from 1940 was re-launched by Onecollection in 2001.*

▼ *Invite as much natural light into your living room as possible, avoid covering up the windows with heavy curtains, and use plenty of lamps for additional illumination.*

Case study

Designer Pella Hedeby > **Year(s)** 2016 > **Place** Stockholm, Sweden

You immediately notice the simplicity of this living room: the natural light coming through the large, floor-to-ceiling windows; the colour scheme, all natural with soft colours; and variation in materials, from wool and wood, to leather, glass and ceramics. This is a true case study on how to do Scandinavian style in your living room.

The most important thing to remember is don't overdo anything when it comes to selecting the furniture and colour scheme. A comfy couch, coffee table and an accent chair can elevate a space without making a huge investment, and are also all you need to make a welcoming living room for you and your guests.

Rather than one large table, group together smaller coffee tables for flexibility. Neutral tones are ideal for big items, such as sofas, tables, armchairs and a rug. Add bolder colours using decorative accessories, such as books and vases.

The sofa will be a statement piece, but you don't want it to take up the entire space. Rather, it should complement the room. Choose a neutral-coloured couch, such as the EJ Delphi Sofa by Erik Jørgensen.

Tables The tables are both made by Danish manufacturer Erik Jørgensen. One has a granite top and the other a white marble top, which has a complementary effect.

Cushions It can be easy to overdo things with cushions on the sofa. Choose designs in simple, single colours, but mix up the fabrics.

Rug A large wool rug with a bold pattern helps pull the room together, gives character and makes the space feel generally more inviting.

Lamps You should have plenty of lamps, ideally one in each corner. Place them strategically, according to where you would need light for reading or using a laptop or tablet. Both lamps here are designed by Arne Jacobsen and manufactured by Louis Poulsen.

Books A small selection of coffee-table books is an easy way to decorate and bring interest to the living room.

Accessories When grouping smaller accessories, such as vases and candleholders, on your coffee table, a good tip is to always go with an uneven number of items – it looks less staged.

Signature colours

Living rooms are the perfect space to relax and unwind after a long day. Colours such as grey, beige and white help to create a calm environment. To create a living room that is full of light and space, use the palest colour on the largest surface area, such as the walls, and darker tones on the furniture.

To create the illusion that your ceiling is higher than it is, use the same colour on the woodwork and walls, as this will make the walls appear taller. Both the graphic black painted framework of the windows and the sheer white curtains enhance the light feel of the room.

The use of darker colours on the sofa and armchair when paired with a beige rug makes the walls appear lighter in contrast. Pale wooden floors, mirrors and glass-topped coffee tables are frequently used in Scandinavian interiors to reflect light, and this increases the airy feel.

To create a contemporary Scandinavian aesthetic, introduce accent colours in the sofa cushions, such as mustard and blue. This is also an easy way to update your interior, as cushion covers can be changed when different colours and patterns become fashionable. Include furniture that has a mixture of wood, chrome, glass and brass. The dark stone grey in the armchair contrasts well with the pale wood and chrome, while the grey and white throw adds pattern and texture to create a modern Scandinavian interior.

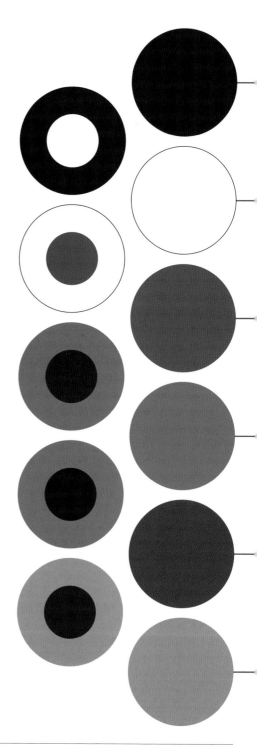

BeoSound 1 and 2

In 1925, Peter Bang and Svend Olufsen founded electronics company Bang & Olufsen, and, like many of their contemporaries, they were highly influenced by the Bauhaus movement. Since then, this Danish firm has produced many of the best-designed sound systems, radios and TVs.

The company is famous not only for its elegant designs but also for its optimal sound; the values of high-end form and function are an important part of modern Scandinavian interiors. In 2016, Torsten Valeur designed a new family of wireless multi-room speakers for the home. While Scandinavian style allows the TV to have a central place in the living room, the speakers should not be too prominent. The minimalist design and portability of both BeoSound 1 and 2 (pictured) allows them to blend into the interior without compromising the sound experience.

Designer
Torsten Valeur

Manufacturer
Bang & Olufsen

Year
2016

Place
Denmark

Material(s)
Aluminium

Dimensions
Beosound 1:
Height: 32.7 cm
Width: 16.2 cm
Depth: 16.2 cm

Beosound 2 (pictured):
Height: 43.1 cm
Width: 19.6 cm
Depth: 19.6 cm

Scandinavian Style at Home

OSLO chair

The OSLO chair, produced by Muuto, is the
embodiment of Scandinavian chic. Designed by
Anderssen & Voll, it is part of a furniture series
that includes two sofas and a pouf. The chair
features a stylish and comfortable seat, delicate
legs and high-quality upholstery from Kvadrat.
It is a great addition to the updated and modern
Scandinavian interior.

The chair feels organic and has a light and
inviting appearance, without compromising on
comfort. It is made on the west coast of Norway
and its embracing and rounded softness reflects
the Nordic warmth that characterizes the designs
of Muuto.

Muuto is rooted in the Scandinavian design
tradition characterized by enduring aesthetics,
functionality and artistry. Its founders, Peter
Bonnén and Kristian Byrge, use innovative
materials and techniques, and work with the
best Nordic designers to create bold and
outstanding furniture and lighting.

Designer
Anderssen & Voll

Manufacturer
Muuto

Year
2013

Place
Denmark

Material(s)
Steel inner frame; Nozag springs;
steel legs with powder-coated surface;
fabric from Kvadrat

Dimensions
Height: 78 cm
Length: 80 cm
Depth: 78 cm

Retreat sofa

Retreat is a modular, flexible sofa system created by Monica Förster for Swedish company Fogia. The design is characterized by cushions that wrap over the armrests and back; it consists of different modules such as single, side and corner seats, and narrow and wide chaises longues. This means the sofas can work in small and large areas, and both colours and fabrics can be changed. Förster says, 'The idea is to give the impression of a padded cover flowing softly from the armrest to the seat, giving the feeling of comfort and softness thus creating a warm atmosphere.'

One of Sweden's leading designers, Förster is internationally renowned for creating functional design with a poetic twist. Her designs are characterized by a sophisticated, unfussy simplicity, and she likes to work with new materials and processes.

Designer
Monica Förster Design Studio

Manufacturer
Fogia

Year
2015

Place
Sweden

Material(s)
Upholstered sofa; solid beech frame

Dimensions
Height: 72 cm
(other dimensions vary)

String® shelving

The simple but elegant shelving system String®
was designed in 1949 by Nils Strinning. The side
panels are made from metal, giving it a light and
airy look, and the shelves can be made from
natural or painted wood.

Bonnier, one of Sweden's largest publishing
houses, realized that if people were to begin
purchasing books in the 1940s, they would need
somewhere to keep them. They held a competition
to find a shelf that had to be affordable, simple to
transport and easy to assemble. Just such a shelf
had existed in the mind of Nils Strinning, and he
won first prize.

Soon after, shelves were ordered for the UN
Building in New York, and five years later, String®
was awarded the gold medal at the Triennale in
Milan. Over the decades, new additions, fittings
and colours have been launched, making it one
of the most versatile shelving systems. It can
easily be used in every room throughout the
Scandinavian-styled home.

Designer
Nils Strinning

Manufacturer
string furniture

Year
1949

Place
Sweden

Material(s)
Powder-coated metal; various woods
(oak, ash or walnut)

Dimensions
Various

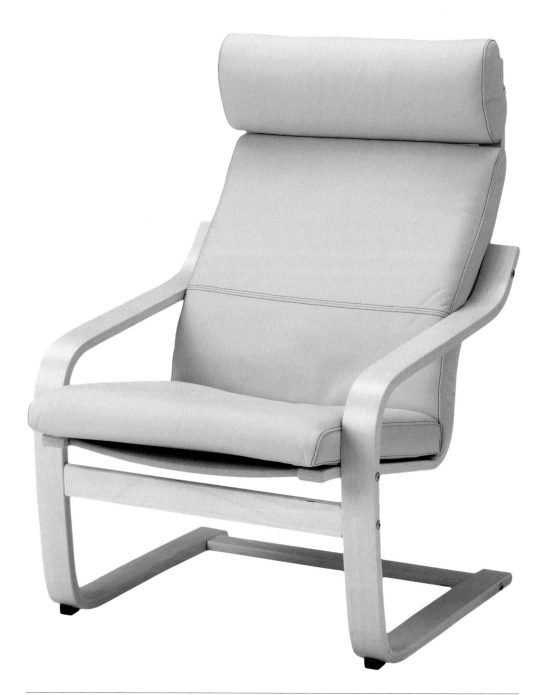

POÄNG chair

Introduced in 1976, the POÄNG chair is arguably one of IKEA's most popular pieces. Japanese designer Noboru Nakamura designed it while employed at IKEA. The chair's curvy design was probably heavily influenced by Alvar Aalto's iconic armchair 406 from 1939, with its bent-birch frame, wavy arms and soft tan upholstery. But where the Aalto chair has a webbed or caned seat, the POÄNG's seat is upholstered and comes in different colours.

Originally, this chair was called POEM, but in 1992 the seat was changed from tubular steel to an all-wood frame. This resulted in a price reduction, and the chair became a self-assembly item, which made it more accessible and popular.

IKEA has produced more than thirty million POÄNG chairs. Its appeal continues today, as it appears in many Scandinavian-style interiors around the world.

Designer
Noboru Nakamura

Manufacturer
IKEA

Year
1976

Place
Sweden

Material(s)
Moulded layer-glued wood veneer with surface of birch veneer; covers available in a variety of fabrics, including leather (seen here)

Dimensions
Height: 100 cm
Seat height: 42 cm
Width: 68 cm
Depth: 82 cm

Penguin lounge chair

Many will recognize the Ant and Swan chairs by Arne Jacobsen, but few will be familiar with the Penguin, designed by Danish furniture designer Ib Kofod-Larsen. While Jacobsen's chairs sold well and became popular features in Scandinavian homes, in the 1950s the Penguin became more popular in the US, where it in fact sold more than the Ant and Swan did back in Denmark.

The Penguin chair has a veneer back in oak, walnut or teak, and a seat upholstered in leather. This light and modern design was first produced by the US furniture company Selig in 1953, but has recently gone back into production by Brdr. Petersens Polstermøbelfabrik, a small Danish studio run by two skilled brothers, Egon & Erling Petersen.

At the time, Ib Kofod-Larsen's designs were not produced by Danish manufacturers, which is perhaps why he didn't receive the same recognition as his more famous colleagues, such as Hans J. Wegner and Børge Mogensen. The Penguin chair is very different from the lighter wooden chairs of the period, which gives it a more contemporary look while retaining that timeless modern style. The lounge chair or rocking chair versions would make a great feature in a modern Scandinavian-style living room – it is also available as a dining chair.

Designer
Ib Kofod-Larsen

Manufacturer
Brdr. Petersens Polstermøbelfabrik

Year
1953

Place
Denmark

Material(s)
SoftArt® Vacona® aniline leather; oak, teak or walnut veneer; powder-coated steel

Dimensions
Height: 74 cm
Width: 55 cm
Depth: 64 cm

COOKING

The kitchen

In Scandinavian homes, the kitchen is often the most important room in the house. This has its roots in the Scandinavian way of living, where inviting friends and family for a meal is a regular occurrence. Food tends to be prepared at home on a daily basis, rather than using convenience foods. No matter the size, the kitchen is a place to enjoy a slower way of life, a place to indulge in all-day cooking and early morning coffee making.

Technology and appliances

Technological advances have brought modern gadgets into the kitchen. This change is also reflected in the design and choice of materials. Straight lines and minimalism are key in the Scandinavian-style kitchen, which means that most appliances are built in and hidden, with the drawers and cabinets having the same fronts.

Storage

With more appliances also comes the need for more storage. When remodelling your kitchen, you have to think ahead. It is actually very simple: no matter how much storage you have in a kitchen, it is never enough! So, do not reduce storage space. Instead, add as much as you can while keeping the style minimalistic and airy. Adding a few extra centimetres to the depth of your cupboards and drawers can create more space. Many Scandinavian kitchens utilize every centimetre from countertops to the floor. If extra centimetres are not an option, open shelving works better than closed cupboards. Embrace Scandinavian style by adding a vintage-style shelf or an old wooden chopping block.

▲ *The minimalist approach in the Scandinavian-style kitchen means that most appliances are built in and hidden, with the drawers and cabinets having uniform fronts.*

▶ *Storage is essential to any kitchen. Add as much as you can, but aim to keep a clean, minimalistic style.*

Prefabricated or made to measure

Kitchens come in all sizes and in every price range. In the cheaper range, IKEA has become a major player when it comes to prefabricated kitchens. Other companies have made it their mission to redesign the IKEA kitchen, making it look like a high-end designer kitchen. In 2013, Swedish company Superfront began manufacturing fronts and handles to fit the most common cabinets. Soon after, Danish company Reform started working with internationally renowned architects to design their kitchens, for example Bjarke Ingels and Norm Architects, making them a household name in Scandinavia and in the US.

At the other end of the spectrum, handmade and long-lasting kitchens have also become popular in Scandinavia. During the financial crises of the 2000s, people started nesting again, which meant spending more time at home and cooking in the kitchen, resulting in more attention being focused on this domestic space.

Materials

Picture the typical Scandinavian-style kitchen, and you are probably thinking of white walls and Corian or wood counters. For many years, these were staples of Scandinavian style, but over time, new materials such as tombac on unit fronts and concrete as countertops have been introduced, while the once prevalent Corian counters have decreased in popularity.

While wooden fronts and countertops are the choice for most in a typical Scandinavian kitchen, using stone tiles as a splash back, for an entire wall, or on the floor, is a great way to add different materials and texture.

The modern Scandinavian kitchen is no longer all white with white countertops. While white is still the dominant colour, grey tones can be combined with materials such as wood, stone, stainless steel, brass and copper. These natural materials add warmth, authenticity and personality to the kitchen decor. The Scandinavian-style kitchen's interior has become post-minimalist.

Countertops

Choosing the right countertop for your kitchen is an important decision, because not only does it set the style for your kitchen, but also it can be expensive. For a Scandinavian-style kitchen, you need to consider not just the overall look, but also its functionality and practicality. Solid wood has been a popular choice for decades; it adds warmth and a natural feel. Other materials to consider include linoleum, marble, concrete, stainless steel and Corian (less common now, but still a good material for a countertop).

▼ *A white marble countertop is both functional and practical, and looks amazing in any kitchen.*

Lighting

Built-in spotlights in the ceiling might be practical, but they have decreased in popularity along with the all-white kitchen of the 1990s. Lamps come in all shapes and sizes, but choose one that provides you with a decent light source for when preparing meals.

Lamps in blown glass are easier to clean and give a soft, yet workable, light. The Swedish company Form Us With Love's Form Pendant lights from 2012 are influenced by industrial light bulbs, which are often seen in Scandinavian-style kitchens. Mid-century lights are also popular. The Danish company Made by Hand produces A. Wedel-Madsen's workshop lamp from 1951. Its solid and industrial look represents urban and minimalistic Scandinavian design in many ways.

▲ *A rack is a clever way to save space and display utensils; it is also an effective way to add visual interest to an all-white kitchen.*

Fittings

Throughout the 1990s and 2000s, Scandinavian kitchens eliminated all fittings, and manufacturers introduced touch-open cupboards. However, adding fittings is a great way to introduce new materials, and an easy and cheap way to update your kitchen. Trends come and go but a kitchen is not easy to replace. If one year brass is fashionable, and the next it is rose gold, you can just change the fittings, and your kitchen feels like new. Tricks like these are very common in the Scandinavian lifestyle.

▲ At Danish kitchen furniture store Reform, internationally renowned architects design fronts for IKEA kitchens that make them look custom-made.

◀ A. Wedel-Madsen's workshop lamp from 1951 has been reproduced by Made by Hand since 2004.

Case study

Designer/Owner Pernilla Algede/House of Beatniks > **Year(s)** 2017 > **Place** Gothenburg, Sweden

The all-white kitchen look has been a popular choice over the last few decades, and it is still the most common one in the Scandinavian style. In older apartments in cities, you will often see that the original kitchen has been maintained and simply updated with a fresh layer of paint. The kitchen here is an example of that. The old units have been given a fresh coat of light-grey paint, and a new marble countertop, white metro tiles on the walls and new modern lamps give a contemporary feel.

Scandinavian Style at Home

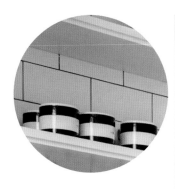

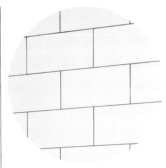

Open shelving *This is a great way to display favourite ceramic pieces and cookware. They have been carefully selected and neatly arranged for a de-cluttered effect.*

Walls *White metro tiled walls such as these have been a favourite in Scandinavian-style kitchens for many years. They are hard-wearing and easy to clean.*

Switches *If you are lucky enough to find an apartment with the original switches, such as these, keep and embrace them. You can also buy modern switches with a vintage look. Make them stand out by choosing black.*

Racks *These racks save space and are a great way to display utensils, placing the cooking tools in the most convenient place.*

Lighting *Artemide's Tolomeo Micro wall lamps, designed by Giancarlo Fassina and Michele de Lucchi, can be directed to a specific spot on the counter to help you see what you are doing. They are also easy to clean.*

Artwork *It can be hard to show your personality in a kitchen, but this colourful painting does the trick.*

Signature colours

While a typical Scandinavian-style kitchen most likely would be an all-white one, wood, especially oak, is becoming more frequently a material of choice in the stand-out high-end kitchen. This handmade kitchen has fronts of knot oak, which, in combination with the white marble countertop, gives it a lively, organic and eye-catching appeal.

The subtle tones are the ideal base for achieving the perfect Scandinavian look – further earthy colours have been added by displaying copper and brass pots and pans, and choosing brass taps and fittings. Brass details work really well with almost any material; even if you choose an all-white or grey kitchen, brass will make the kitchen pop and add personality.

Green is another colour that works well with the predominantly neutral colour scheme preferred in Scandinavian style. The obvious way to get green into your kitchen is by adding plants, as has been done here. As you want your kitchen to be a place of life and a place where there is room for cooking, small plants add a natural vibe to the clean surface – with an extra practical bonus if you choose herbs that can be used in your cooking.

A narrow rug not only makes the kitchen look bigger, but also adds texture and a bit of extra colour to the all-white floor. Grey is one of the most dominant colours in the Scandinavian style, so no room should be without it.

Tools utensils

The Tools range was designed by Björn Dahlström in 1998. The Swedish-born designer developed a range of cooking utensils in collaboration with a professional chef for the Finnish manufacturer Hackman (today produced by littala). The brief was to produce something both beautiful and durable, which are fundamental values of Scandinavian style.

The final pieces resulted in professional-quality oven-to-tableware pots. The elegant forms of the cookware and its understated, matt, brushed-steel finish means that you want it on show.

The functional feature of the Tools range is a sandwich technique that allows aluminium to be encased in stainless steel. Aluminium has excellent heat distribution properties and the stainless steel is used to protect the user from any of the damaging properties of aluminium, the steel also makes it more hard-wearing.

Björn Dahlström is a leading contemporary designer known internationally for his work in furniture and industrial design. Dahlström's designs are known for their stark graphics and the distinct way that they express soft and fundamental forms.

Designer
Björn Dahlström

Manufacturer
littala

Year
1998

Place
Finland

Material(s)
Aluminium, encased in stainless steel

Dimensions
Various

Würtz tableware

Würtz tableware was designed by Aage and Kasper Würtz in 2006. In Scandinavian-style kitchens, handmade tableware is used increasingly. This trend has been influenced by the growing popularity of new Nordic cuisine following the success of restaurants such as Geranium, Noma and Amass in Copenhagen, and Törst and Luksus located in New York, which frequently use this kind of tableware.

These pieces have been described as showing signature characteristics of the designers' work: 'an assured inner–outer ratio, a subtle concavity even in the flattest dinner plates, unexpected rims, moody colorations, random flecked and mottled surface effects...' These types of colour and shape for tableware are popular today in new Nordic and Scandinavian-style homes.

Aage and Kasper Würtz are a father-and-son team of ceramists. They are well known for their hand-thrown, hand-glazed pieces, created using ancient wheel-turning and glazing techniques. They work with stoneware and porcelain, and their pieces are available from K. H. Würtz.

Designer
Aage and Kasper Würtz

Manufacturer
K. H. Würtz

Year
2006

Place
Denmark

Material(s)
Hand-thrown, hand-glazed stoneware

Dimensions
Various

Cylinda Line coffee pot

The Cylinda Line coffee pot was designed by Arne Jacobsen in 1967. As we have already seen, Jacobsen is one of the most versatile and recognized Danish architects, who designed not just buildings but also everyday objects. With its clean lines and attractive cylindrical shape, this coffee pot has become a Scandinavian-style icon. It can be used for serving coffee or hot chocolate.

The classic AJ coffee pot was one of the first designs in the Cylinda Line range and was the piece that put the relatively unknown Danish brand Stelton on the map. This was modern, cutting-edge design of its day, clearly influenced by minimalism. Since its introduction, Stelton has added more pieces to the range, such as a press-top coffee maker to cater for the contemporary market.

In 2017, the fiftieth anniversary of Cylinda Line was celebrated with the launch of special-edition versions featuring beautifully coloured enamel. The colours have been carefully chosen in recognition of Jacobsen's colour schemes, and inspired by his work with watercolours, textiles and carpets.

Designer
Arne Jacobsen

Manufacturer
Stelton

Year
1967

Place
Denmark

Material(s)
18/8 stainless steel; Bakelite handle

Dimensions
Height: 27 cm
Width: 25 cm
Depth: 16 cm

Perfection red wine glass

The Perfection wine glass was designed by Tom Nybroe in 2006. Nybroe is a wine enthusiast, and he wanted to design the perfect wine glass. The shape of the glass makes it comfortable to hold. The bend in the glass helps in pouring the correct amount of wine up to the widest point; it is here that the wine has the best conditions needed for developing its flavour.

As well as being a wine enthusiast, Nybroe is also an advertising executive, graphic designer and wine importer. The design of the glass was based on research with professional sommeliers and wine producers worldwide to produce the best vessel for appreciating wine. The glass was created for Holmegaard, one of Denmark's most prestigious glass manufacturers.

Designer
Tom Nybroe

Manufacturer
Holmegaard

Year
2006

Material(s)
Glass

Dimensions
Height: 22 cm
Width: 8 cm
Depth: 8 cm

EATING

The dining room

▲ *Entertaining friends and family around a dining table is something that Scandinavians do often.*

▶ *Decorate the walls in your dining room with something that will help tell a story to your guests; for example, you could include a map of your favourite city.*

The use of clean lines, elegant curves and neutral tones will create a stunning Scandinavian-style dining room. Furniture in natural wood and soft white is a good starting point for a dining area. Bear in mind who will actually use the dining space. If you have friends with children, you might want to consider a play area, but if you are solely planning on hosting fine-dining parties, you probably just need a large table.

Many homes do not have a separate dining room, so if you have an open-plan living space, it will incorporate your dining area. Here, the dining table sits at the heart of a home, acting as a gathering point where family members, friends and guests meet. So the table that stands in the living room, kitchen or family room carries a great deal of emotional weight. It needs to be functional and durable enough to support family life, and it should be inviting to your guests.

The choice of furniture is the most important element of the dining space. Place the table and chairs in the centre so that they are the focal point; the decorative elements play a minor role in the general scheme. The simplicity keeps the emphasis on the food and the company.

The colours used in a Scandinavian-style dining room are mostly white, dark grey and light grey. With touches of black, when mixed with wooden elements, provide a tranquil feel.

Dining table

Some Scandinavian dining tables are inspired by mid-century and classic styles, while others have interpreted these designs in an updated and modern way. Most Scandinavian-style dining tables are made of wood. This is an easy way to incorporate nature into the dining room, and there is nothing that says Scandinavian style more

▲ *Poul Henningsen's iconic PH 5*
pendant lamp is designed to provide
a completely glare-free light.

than long, solid wooden planks. A wooden table has been a part of Scandinavian life for decades, so there are many well-known brands that

manufacture them. If the dining room does not allow for a long rectangular table, oval or circular shapes might suit your space better. For example, the Super-Elliptical table designed in 1968 is based on Piet Hein's super-elliptical roundabout in Stockholm. If your budget doesn't allow for one of the mid-century classics, consider the simple Loop Stand by Hay introduced in 2002, which allows you to change the top as often as you want.

Marble has started to make a comeback in Scandinavian design. For example, Poul Kjærholm's iconic PK54 table is a work of art in which stone meets steel; while Emil Thorup for Handvärk introduced his version of a slim, sleek marble table.

Dining chairs

For many years, a simple farmhouse table paired with white Eames DSW chairs was the epitome of Scandinavian style. Scandinavians loved the Eames chair as if it was one of their own, but slowly new designs for chairs have been introduced. You can divide people into two groups. One group have replaced their Eames chairs with another mid-century chair, such as Wegner's Wishbone chair designed in 1949 or Arne Jacobsens's Series 7™ chair from 1955.

The other group went new Nordic, choosing from many quickly growing dining chair collections. Since 2010, every major Scandinavian designer has launched at least one new version of the dining chair. In 2013, Muuto produced the Cover chair by Thomas Bentzen, and two years later Simon Legald launched his chair called Form with Normann Copenhagen. Both chairs express the classic Scandinavian design values of simplicity, natural materials and craftsmanship.

▼ *The round version of the Loop Stand dining table, made by Hay since 2002, is a suitable solution for smaller spaces.*

Lighting

Lighting is the final key element of every Scandinavian-style dining room. Good lighting allows diners to see and experience their food at its best. Brighter light may be needed for activities like homework and board games, but avoid blinding people as they sit round the table.

Metal lamps that hang directly above the table focus the light downward, which gives the illusion of pulling the space together. Glass lights with a more diffused light illuminate the entire room. A classic, popular lamp is the PH 5 designed by Poul Henningsen in 1958; it is said there is one in every other Danish home.

Match the number of lights you have to the size of your dining table. You can choose either one big statement light, such as the PH Artichoke lamp (see pages 64–65), or two smaller lamps, or perhaps a group of lights to create a modern chandelier effect.

Additional decoration

Dining room adornments are kept to a minimum; one large or a few colourful art pieces and green plants in the window are all it takes to decorate a Scandinavian-style dining room. It is important that your guests have something to look at when you are preparing the food, but the food should be the centre of attention.

▲ *Round tables are a more efficient use of space, making them ideal for small rooms or creating a dining area in part of an open-plan room.*

◄ *The Cover chair, designed by Thomas Bentzen for Muuto, is a new classic for the Scandinavian-style dining room.*

Case study

Designer/Owner Anonymous > **Year(s)** 2017 > **Place** Gothenburg, Sweden

Attention to detail is just as important in the dining room as in all the other rooms in the Scandinavian style. Clean lines, simple shapes and neutral tones are all it takes to achieve a stunning Scandinavian-style dining room like this one. The colours are kept neutral in a mix of white, dark and light grey, and black mixed with wooden hues, making it a very calm and welcoming dining room. Black-painted mid-century chairs are mixed perfectly with a new wooden table and lit by an almost cloudlike lamp, surrounded by light-grey walls, lots of natural light from the big window, all pulled together by a grey woollen rug.

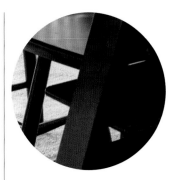

Table *The Scandinavian-style dining table is usually made of wood, such as the one shown here in light, solid oak. The size of the table will often be as big as the room allows, so that you can entertain family and friends.*

Chairs *The pale wood of the table and the black-painted wooden chairs create an interesting contrast. This design is inspired by that of the Danish architect and designer Poul M. Volther, from the 1960s. It produces a natural but elegant look.*

Baby chair *The baby highchair at the end of the table is the iconic Tripp Trapp, made by Norwegian manufacturer Stokke and designed by Peter Opsvik in 1972.*

Lamp *The wide paper lampshade, reminiscent of George Nelson's iconic Bubble Lamp from 1947, works well above the dining table. It softens and diffuses the light on and around diners.*

Tableware *Handmade tableware has become very popular. The elegant and simple shapes seen here reflect the clean lines of Scandinavian style.*

Picture *A colourful picture is the easiest way to incorporate colour into your dining room – and a great conversation starter.*

Signature colours

The dining area can be the heart of a Scandinavian home; whether used as a place for the family to meet or as a room for entertaining and dinner parties, the decor sets the scene.

To create a sophisticated but natural look in a small dining area, consider layering neutral colours to give the scheme depth. The sheer white curtains against the cold white tiles help to create an intimate and warm feel. The rustic wooden table contrasts well with the Eames DSW chairs (shown here) with their white organic-shaped seats and clean, modern legs. The lampshade above the table adds texture and interest that coordinates well with the stark smooth tiles.

In this informal dining room, the accent colour is the pale blue used on the floor. Painting the floor in this chequered combination of light blue and white adds a hint of colour without dominating the space. You can use tiles to produce the same effect. The classic colours create a timeless Scandinavian feel and, when used in this way, can make the room appear larger, which is useful in a small dining area.

Keep strong and bright colours to a minimum in a small space, but if you have a large dining area, do not leave them out completely. They can create a dramatic, intimate atmosphere that is perfect for entertaining. Some colour on the floor, in the curtains or in a painting (choose one of these options, not all of them) works especially well in dining rooms that are lit by candlelight. Rich, velvety tones are intensified by candlelight and take on a wonderful jewel-like quality.

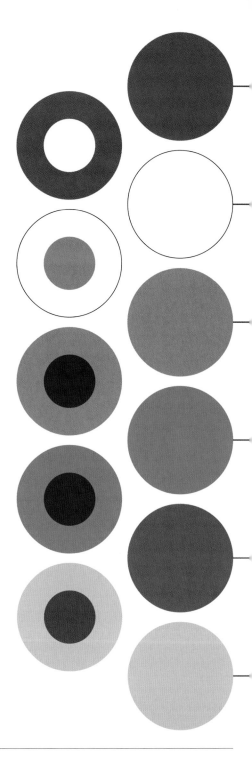

Beetle chair

The Beetle chair was designed by Danish/Italian design duo Stine Gam and Enrico Fratesi in 2013. As you may have guessed, the inspiration for the Beetle chair came from the eponymous creature. They reinterpreted the beetle's anatomy with its hard shell and characteristic shape into a chair design. The chair is elegant and comfortable, and works well in formal and informal dining spaces. It comes in a plastic shell version, in seven different colours and in a variety of fully upholstered versions with trimmings around the side of the seat and either a thin, powder-coated chrome, brass or wooden base. The upholstered version is extremely comfortable, making it ideal around the dining table for long dinners with friends and family.

Design partnership GamFratesi exemplifies the union of Danish and Italian design principles. The minimal approach of Scandinavian design is combined with a sense of quirkiness. With GamFratesi, the contrasts are often key to their inspiration. They work strictly within the Scandinavian approach to craft, simplicity and functionalism, but there is a strong emotional pull in the story behind each piece.

Since its launch, the Beetle chair has become popular with interior designers all over the world. This chair is very different from the wooden mid-century chairs often seen in the Scandinavian-style dining room, and that is deliberate: GamFratesi is making a statement that Scandinavian design is not only from the 1940s and 1950s.

Designer
Stine Gam and Enrico Fratesi

Manufacturer
Gubi

Year
2013

Place
Denmark

Material(s)
Various; fully upholstered, customized by choice of fabric, colour and base (wood, brass, black chrome or black-painted steel)

Dimensions
Height: 83 cm
Width: 52 cm
Depth: 53.5 cm

Blown lamp

Blown is a mouth-blown pendant lamp with a quilted pattern designed by Samuel Wilkinson for the Danish company &tradition in 2013. The designer researched the many ways light reflects and refracts off different materials. The resulting glass shade, with a quilted texture that is inspired by raspberries, produces a soft and playful light effect. Hang a single one or a cluster of three or more above the dining table for a perfect ambient atmosphere.

The London-based designer Samuel Wilkinson was already winning awards before he opened his industrial design studio in 2008. He had created design-consultancy projects for British Airways, Audi, Samsung and Virgin Airways before moving onto furniture and industrial design. He has pieces in permanent collections at MoMA and the Cooper-Hewitt, Smithsonian Design Museum in New York, and the Victoria & Albert Museum in London.

Designer
Samuel Wilkinson

Manufacturer
&tradition

Year
2013

Place
Denmark

Material(s)
Mouth-blown glass; powder-coated metal suspension

Dimensions
Height: 28 cm
Diameter: 28 cm

Essay™ table

The Essay™ table was designed by Cecilie Manz in 2009. It consists of three elements: a tabletop and two bases. Its construction looks natural and elegant. The table is also extremely functional and flexible; it can be expanded by using the black linoleum leavers. This is particularly useful if your table is used not just for eating but for other purposes – the clutter can be pushed aside to allow space for dining.

Cecilie Manz's Scandinavian style is reflected in her respect for materials, durability and simplicity. The table is indicative of her approach, with its simple lines and sparse form that is softened by its smooth, rounded legs. An elegant design made from solid wood, this table is firm and hard-wearing but also light enough not to dominate a room.

Cecilie Manz is one of the leading Danish furniture designers of her generation. This table was designed for Fritz Hansen, but she has also produced work for Lightyears, Holmegaard and Muuto.

Designer
Cecilie Manz

Manufacturer
Fritz Hansen

Year
2009

Place
Denmark

Material(s)
Solid wood (oak, ash,
black-coloured ash or walnut)

Dimensions
Height: 72 cm
Length: 265 cm
Width: 100 cm

Kubus candleholder

The Kubus candleholder was designed by
Mogens Lassen in 1962. It makes a classic
Scandinavian-style centrepiece for a dining table,
because of its simple form and use of materials.
It is available in lacquered metal in black or white,
brass-plated metal, copper-plated metal (shown
here) and nickel-plated metal. Its different versions
can hold one to eight candles.

It was originally produced for his family and
design colleagues, but has since become a
design classic. In 2008, Nadia Lassen, Mogens's
great-grandchild, started the company By Lassen,
and Kubus established itself as an iconic piece of
Scandinavian style.

The candleholder is found in many homes
across Scandinavia and has become increasingly
popular. In December 2014, more than 1,000
pieces were sold every day.

Designer
Mogens Lassen

Manufacturer
By Lassen

Year
1962

Place
Denmark

Material(s)
Untreated copper-plated metal

Dimensions
Height: 23 cm
Width: 23 cm

Vilda 2 chair

The Vilda chair was designed by Jonas Bohlin in 2012. The simple and light form and the use of natural material of the original Vilda chair perfectly reflect Scandinavian style, and the chair has quickly become a new classic.

It is manufactured using an old Swedish technique, bending solid beech or ash, which makes the chair extremely durable. It is ecologically sound, as the wood comes from certified forests. The Vilda 2 chair has an open back constructed from one long piece of wood bent into shape, wrapped in leather for added comfort. Other models of the chair have been fitted with larger pieces of leather for extra back support. All chairs come only in the raw beech or ash wood tone, but with five different colours of leather.

The chair is the result of a forty-year-long interest between the designer and his love of bent wood. While studying at Konstfack (Sweden's largest university of design, arts and crafts), Bohlin visited Gemla, Sweden's oldest furniture factory located in the heart of the old forests of Småland. He was immediately fascinated by the process of how the bent wood forms resulted in delicate furniture. Decades later, Bohlin's earlier experiences with the bent-wood technique resulted in the Vilda 2 Chair.

Designer
Jonas Bohlin

Manufacturer
Gemla

Year
2012

Place
Sweden

Material(s)
Ash, leather

Dimensions
Height: 89 cm
Width: 41 cm
Depth: 54 cm

CLEANSING

The bathroom

Minimalist design is the most instantly recognizable feature of any Scandinavian-style bathroom. The clean lines, smooth edges and simple but functional layout are the three elements at the heart of every minimalist bathroom design. While the rest of the Scandinavian-style home has slowly begun to incorporate colours, after a long period where everything was minimalistic and white, the Scandinavian bathroom is still all about clean, crisp white.

Up until the 1990s, green and brown featured in the Scandinavian-style bathroom, even tiles with flowers, but following the financial boom in the 2000s, many bathrooms were renovated into what is now recognized as the modern Scandinavian bathroom. These days, bathrooms are much more than just a space for a quick pit stop. It is a room to promote well-being.

A simple way to achieve the minimalist look is to choose white bathroom tiles and fittings. Fixtures typically include brushed stainless steel or polished chrome. The toilet and basin are always white. Another reason to have an all-white bathroom is that it is easier to maintain and appears more hygienic.

The finishing touches should include a stool, bench or chair, and a surface to put your towels, magazines and candles.

Calm, neutral tones

The colours for the Scandinavian-style bathroom are white, combined with tones of grey and cream. These neutral colours create a calm, muted feel. Accent colours can be incorporated through accessories and towels. Indulge your individual style by using colour-coordinated bathroom sets, towels and accessories.

▲ *The Scandinavian-style bathroom should feel like entering a spa, projecting a sense of well-being.*

▶ *As with other rooms in the home, the popular colour scheme for the Scandinavian-style bathroom is white combined with grey tones.*

Beautiful tiled floors

Carpet is a material you will never see in a Scandinavian-style bathroom. To create a beautiful floor, use tiles. The best colours to choose are white, cream and light grey. Place tiles in different patterns and sizes on the floor and the walls.

Natural light

Scandinavian-style bathrooms make the most of light. As winter in Scandinavia is long and dark, the design style has reacted to this seasonal weather by making the best use of natural light.

A big part of what makes Scandinavian-style bathrooms feel so relaxing is the natural light entering through windows. Stay clear of dark and heavy window shades and blinds that will block sunlight from filling the bathroom. Installing light fixtures such as pendants or wall lights will not only add a modern flare, but also keep your bathroom bright even when the sun sets.

Large bathroom mirrors and reflective surfaces like ceramic tiles are key to making the most of light in the bathroom.

▲ *Most modern Scandinavian-style bathrooms make use of wall-mounted fixtures, as seen here with this mirrored bathroom cabinet.*

Wall fixtures

Wall-hung fixtures have been used in Scandinavian-style bathrooms for many years. Whether you choose to hang all your bathroom fixtures off the wall or just the vanity unit or toilet, wall-hung units are a fantastic way of opening up the space on the bathroom floor. Also, it is much easier to clean a floor that has no units on it.

Danish architect Knud Holscher has designed many objects that most Scandinavians encounter everyday without knowing it. He is behind one of the most recognized wall-hung toilets in Scandinavian-style bathrooms, the Ifö by Geberit, which was inspired by Nordic nature and organic minimalism.

▲ *To maintain a clean look in your Scandinavian bathroom, keep only the essentials displayed and make sure you have enough storage to keep the room clutter-free.*

Case study

Designer/Owner Pernilla Algede/House of Beatniks >

Year(s) 2017 > **Place** Gothenburg, Sweden

In a small bathroom, it is important to stick with the 'less is more' mindset. De-clutter as much as possible and only have what you need on display. Ask yourself: what do I really need and what can I live without? Choose the basin, fixtures and shelving accordingly. This is a classic example of the smaller bathroom, which is very typical in Scandinavia, especially in cities. A simple way to achieve the minimalist look is to choose white bathroom tiles and fittings, but that doesn't always have to be the case. Here, the contrast between the white wall tiles and their black grout creates a clean, crisp effect, while the black toilet seat ties in neatly with this scheme. The vintage brass basin and fixtures provide a quirky element that prevents the overall feel from being clinical.

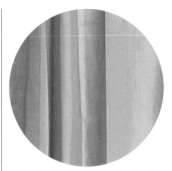

Open shelving *This unit is called string®, designed by Nils Strinning in 1949 (see page 87). It is good for small and narrow bathrooms.*

Shampoo bottles *Neutral-coloured refill bottles have been used here, instead of having several different-coloured ones. This helps to keep the area free from clutter. The Japanese company Muji is a good source for these.*

Shower curtain *The brighter colour of the shower curtain adds an element of fun to this design. Prints have been avoided, however, as this would have made this small bathroom look too busy.*

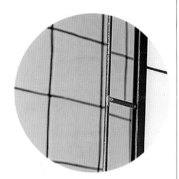

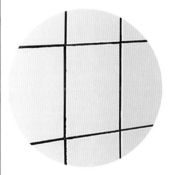

Mirror *This vintage mirror adds character and ties in well with the brass basin.*

Brass basin and tap *Brass ages well and looks amazing while doing so. Unlike chrome, brass does not need constant cleaning in order to look fresh.*

Tiles *White tiles with black grout are commonly used in Scandinavian-style bathrooms.*

Signature colours

Small bathrooms are often decorated with white or light-coloured tiles, making them appear bigger and brighter. This always works; however, it can be tricky not to end up with a dull room that has little character. While most Scandinavian-style bathrooms do have white walls, you can introduce a touch of colour into a bathroom with little or no natural light. Not everything needs to be all-white.

Using warm colours, such as shades of brown and beige, will help to create an intimate space. For a relaxed bathroom, use coloured mosaic tiles. The mosaic tiles on the wall of this bathroom are in a darker tone than the floor tiles, but the use of white grout connects the two and makes the room look fresh.

The pale-coloured tiles behind the bath blend well with the wooden basin unit. The use of wood creates a natural feeling, one of the signature features of Scandinavian style.

The use of white fittings for the basin, bath and toilet keeps the bathroom looking clean and elegant. The white towels and bathmat complement the other white goods and ensure that the room has a calm yet luxurious feel.

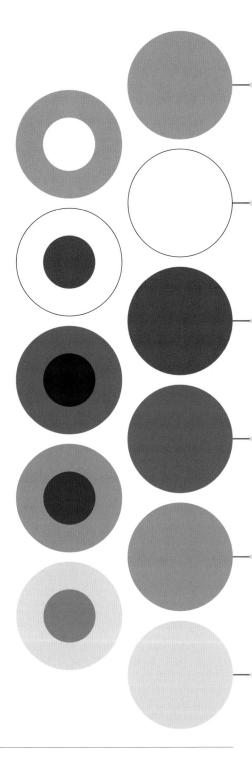

HV1 mixer tap

The HV1 wall-mounted mixer tap was originally designed for the Danish National Bank in 1968 by Arne Jacobsen, one of Denmark's best-known architects and mid-century designers. Today, it is produced by VOLA.

The minimalistic and simple style of the HV1 is very appealing in the clean-lined Scandinavian-style bathroom; you may also see it used in the kitchen. The design is not just stylish; it is simple and functional, allowing the user to adjust the temperature much more efficiently than with a two-tap system.

VOLA continues to develop the HV1, and with a small water-saving device inside the nozzle, the tap configures your needs for the right amount of water, thereby saving you money. The material used in mixers, taps and all inside accessories is solid brass, with some valve housings in dezincification-resistant brass, which makes the taps last a lifetime.

Jacobsen is probably most famous for the chairs he designed: the Egg, the Ant, the Series 7™ and the Swan, which are all produced by Fritz Hansen.

Designer
Arne Jacobsen

Manufacturer
VOLA

Year
1968

Place
Denmark

Material(s)
Solid brass and gun metal; dezincification-resistant brass housings; some stainless-steel components

Dimensions
Height: 12 cm
Width: 13.4 cm
Depth: 4 cm

Vipp pedal bin

The Vipp pedal bin was designed by Holger Nielsen in 1939. It was originally made for his wife Marie's hairdressing salon. Holger trained as a metalsmith, and he wanted to produce a bin that worked well and was durable.

Originally, the Vipp bin was intended for Marie's use only. However, her salon was frequented by many doctors' and dentists' wives who thought the Vipp bin would work well in their husbands' clinics, because of its practical and sturdy design. This pedal bin soon became a permanent fixture in Danish clinics and is still used today. The simple yet striking bin comes in two different colours (black and white), which perfectly suits the modern Scandinavian-style bathroom. The small pedal makes the lid open easily, without you having to touch the bin and dirty your hands. A rubber ring between the lid and bin guarantees air-tight closure, which makes it perfect if you have small children and need to dispose of a lot of nappies. The material makes the bin great for damp bathrooms, as it's easy to wipe clean, and it comes in five different sizes.

Designer
Holger Nielsen

Manufacturer
Vipp

Year
1939

Place
Denmark

Material(s)
Powder-coated steel; rubber and stainless-steel components

Dimensions
(Medium-sized, pictured)
Height: 62 cm
Width: 30 cm
Depth: 30 cm

Over Me light

Over Me is a light designed by Morten Skjærpe Knarrum and Jonas Norheim in 2017. Its minimalist flush-mounted design is elegant and stylish. It consists of a sleek metal frame, a glass disc and a circular shade. The rounded shade casts diffused light from all around. It is particularly suited to bathrooms because it is certified for use in wet areas. It can also be secured to different surfaces and used on the ceiling or attached to a wall, making it versatile and adaptable. If used on a wall, the light can become a focal point, but it is subtle enough to blend in with the ceiling, if required. It is made in two sizes and available in off-white, dusty blue and dark grey – colours that are perfect for a Scandinavian-style bathroom.

The Norwegian designers are based in Bergen, Norway. They are well known for creating quirky cutting-edge lighting and furniture. Morten and Jonas have been successful in elevating their designs, and winning awards as a result. They have created several lamps, including the Over Me ceiling and pendant series for Norwegian lamp manufacturer Northern Lighting.

Designer
Morten Skjærpe Knarrum
and Jonas Norheim

Manufacturer
Northern Lighting

Year
2017

Place
Sweden

Material(s)
Body: steel; shade: glass

Dimensions
Height: 14 cm
Width: 30 cm
Depth: 30 cm

Framed mirror

Framed is a mirror designed by Anderssen & Voll for Muuto in 2016. A mirror is an essential item in a bathroom, for obvious grooming-related reasons. A large mirror can also make a small bathroom appear bigger. Scandinavian-style mirrors tend to be round or oval shaped, or have rounded corners like the Framed mirror. The mirror can be hung in groups of two or more – if you have the space – to create a mirror installation, which is a great way to keep the bathroom feeling light and airy.

The stand-out feature of this design is that it comes in various shades of coloured glass, including rose, grey and taupe. This unusual quality challenges the purely functional status of the mirror, making it a decorative design piece in its own right.

Designer
Anderssen & Voll

Manufacturer
Muuto

Year
2016

Place
Denmark

Material(s)
Powder-coated steel; mirror-glass sheet

Dimensions
Height: 118 cm
Width: 44.5 cm
Depth: 4 cm

Prime bathtub

The Prime bathtub was designed by Norm
Architects in 2017. The simple and functional
Prime series includes two bathtubs and a sink
design that is a modern interpretation of old-
fashioned baths. The soft outer shape was
influenced by how the pressure of water can
mould a flexible material. The organic shape along
with the soft-rolled edge makes the bath visually
appealing and inviting. It is contemporary and
familiar at the same time, which makes it ideal
for a Scandinavian-style bathroom.

Danish designers Norm Architects created this
bath for Spanish manufacturer Inbani. They have
worked with many international companies. This
multidisciplinary design studio strives to create
objects that are elegant, functional and durable
using clean lines that are very much a feature of
Scandinavian style.

Designer
Norm Architects

Manufacturer
Inbani

Year
2017

Place
Spain

Material(s)
Solid surface/Corian

Dimensions
Height: 65.5 cm
Width: 180 cm
Depth: 100 cm

RESTING

The bedroom

A busy family or working life calls for a tranquil space where you can switch off and relax at the end of the day. Scandinavian-style bedrooms are some of the most relaxing spaces you can find. Clutter is banished, and toned-down colours, neat bedding, simple decor and elements of nature create calm and serene spaces.

Bedrooms are often overlooked and not given enough attention in terms of design. However, the bedroom should not be an afterthought. Although the design work for a bedroom is not as intensive as for the bathroom or kitchen, the Scandinavian-style bedroom will nonetheless need some thought in order to get it right.

First consider the key areas: circulation, furniture placement, views, outdoor access, light and ventilation. It is important to think about what you want out of your bedroom. For example, if you read in bed, greater consideration should be given to a comfortable and soft headboard for you to lean back on, a bedside table to hold your books and excellent lighting for reading. Lots of light during the day is very important in the Scandinavian-style bedroom and they typically have large windows. If this is the case with your bedroom, and you like your room to be dark when sleeping, then blackout curtains will be essential.

The bed

The most important element of any bedroom is the bed. We spend one-third of our life lying in bed, so invest in a comfortable. Choose your mattress carefully; seek some professional help with finding the right level of firmness for you.

▲ *Toned-down colours, neat blankets and bedding are some of the key elements of a Scandinavian-style bedroom.*

▶ *Stick to a calm colour scheme, breaking it up a little with splashes of colour and accessories in natural materials.*

▲ This design makes good use of a small space with plenty of storage above and below the bed.

Bed frames are often seen in Scandinavian bedrooms, and if you do opt for a headboard, you need to pick a slim and simple one. A basic, low frame is essential. As Scandinavian bedrooms tend to be small, a bed on legs is popular, as being able to see beneath it adds to the feeling of space. If you are looking for storage space, a bed with drawers underneath helps to create a clutter-free room.

Colours

Scandinavians' bedrooms, like the rest of their interiors, usually have minimal amounts of colour. They are kept natural and bright, and typically use one of two colour schemes.

Scandinavian-style bedrooms sometimes feature all-dark walls, a dark feature wall or richly coloured textiles that give the room a cosy feel and add a sense of depth to the space. More commonly, the colour palette uses white and light tones of grey. This keeps the space feeling airy, while the greys give it a slightly contrasting tone.

Colours have a huge influence in helping our minds relax. As mentioned earlier, the colour scheme in Scandinavian-style bedrooms is typically (although not always – see case study) neutral tones. One way that you may choose to add colour is through artwork. The choice of artwork or print is up to you, but blue, green or neutral tones work best to instil calm. You can cluster a combination of different artworks together, or choose a large feature piece that could be placed above the bed.

Materials

Textiles are another way to achieve Scandinavian style. Drape your bed with chunky knit blankets in layers or textured linen throws for warmth. Soft pillows and cushions piled up at the head of the bed add comfort. And of course, wooden elements, such as a sideboard, low stool or bench, create the perfect mix of textures that add dimension and warmth to the bedroom.

Curtains

Studies show that the darker your bedroom is when you sleep, the deeper and better you sleep, a fact that clashes with the bright and light tones we typically see in Scandinavian-style bedrooms. Sheer curtains might match best with the room but you could consider installing made-to-measure blackout blinds. Combining the two is the best option; use light fabric curtains purely for decoration with a blackout blind behind them.

Bedside tables

Bedside tables are a great style feature, but also very practical. You should keep your side tables uncomplicated so as not to take attention away from the bed. If you have a lot of things, opt for a side table with a drawer. Bedside tables or

▼ *You can break up a natural scheme by painting one wall in a bold colour.*

▲ *Where space or budget is an issue, be flexible; a bedside table could be created from a chair, stool or a small table.*

nightstands in Scandinavian-style bedrooms are usually unique: it's common to find chairs, stools, crates, baskets, or even just piles of magazines used as bedside tables, giving the room a minimal yet functional and somewhat playful feel.

Wardrobe

Not everyone has a spare room for a walk-in closet, but you can easily incorporate a great-looking clothes-storage solution, whether a fitted wardrobe or an open clothing rack.

The downside with an open clothing rack is that it needs to be kept fastidiously tidy at all times to prevent the room looking cluttered. However, if done right, it will put the finishing touch to a perfectly styled bedroom and give it that extra homely and cosy feeling. If you do like to keep your clothes out of sight, a fitted wardrobe is a very good option. Just choose a simple front,

which either flips or slides open.
Make sure it doesn't have too many
embellishments: simplicity is key.

Plants

Plants are one of the elements
of Scandinavian-style. Whether
it is a large house plant sitting
in a corner, a succulent on a
bedside table or dried flowers
in a vase on top of the dresser,
elements of nature are essential.
Plants are not just decorative:
they also help to purify the air.

Indoor plants will instantly
bring your room to life, and you
will never want to leave your
peaceful green indoor sanctuary.
Some plants, such as jasmine,
have a gentle and soothing effect
on your body while you sleep;
others, such as lavender, have
even been shown to reduce
crying in babies. One thing to
remember: don't go full-on
botanical garden in your
bedroom – one or two is plenty.

▶ This bright bedroom is decorated in
cool greys with just a splash of colour
added for character, keeping the overall
style calm and relaxing.

Case study

Designer/Owner Auping > **Year** 2015 > **Place** Frederiksberg, Denmark

Many would describe this particular bedroom as non-Scandinavian. However, there are several classic Scandinavian-style elements: plenty of natural light from the floor-to-ceiling windows; the light-oak herringbone floor; a big floor vase; and a large green plant. The Scandinavian-style bedroom is one room where adding more colour works well, but it needs to be done with purpose, as seen here, and look clutter-free. This bedroom is influenced by southern Europe, with the palm-tree linen and claret-coloured bed frame, which is something increasingly seen in the Scandinavian-style bedroom, as people travel more regularly and want to add a bit of luxurious hotel atmosphere to their bedroom. The bed should take centre stage when you are going for that perfect luxe hotel style. Think of all the hotels that you have visited – they are always well designed with the bed as the main attraction. Notice how the bed linen complements the colour of the headboard – something to bear in mind if you choose to install one.

Bed frame *Dutch bed company Auping's high-end, environmentally friendly beds and mattresses suit Scandinavian style's values of sustainable living.*

Bedside table *Small coffee tables, like this simple brass one, often look much better than typical wooden pieces with a built-in drawer.*

Bed linen *Colourful bedding is okay, as long as the colours are bold and fresh. In this case, the palm-tree linen works because all the other elements are on point for a Scandinavian-style bedroom.*

Light *This Pleat Box lamp is ceramic and handmade by Spanish company Apparatu. The lampshade looks like folded fabric, which adds texture, and the dusky-green colour, with its brass interior, picks up on the colours of the bed linen and the plant.*

Plants *Plants are the ultimate addition to any room and the bedroom is no exception. Make sure you work out what type of light your bedroom receives and choose a plant accordingly. The single, sculptural plant used here is almost a piece of art in itself.*

Floor *The wooden floor gives the bedroom warmth, life and atmosphere. It doesn't get more Scandinavian style than a wooden herringbone floor. If you are lucky enough to have one, don't cover it with rugs.*

Signature colours

Unlike our vibrant case study, this room takes a more typical approach to the Scandinavian-style colour scheme. Neutral colours, like the white and dark grey used in this room, are perfect for creating a relaxed and calming environment in the bedroom. You might choose other muted shades, such as pale greys and blues, which also work really well in creating a soothing effect.

The bare floorboards and the white ceiling work in contrast to the dark grey walls to add a sense of grandness and make the room seem bigger and taller.

Adding accents of colour is a great way to update a bedroom. Here, a subtle hint of green has been added with the plant and the artwork. Choose colours that complement your existing wall colours and use them sparingly to add that 'pop' of colour.

Finally, the brown tones of the bedspread and wooden chest of drawers and chairs add that element of nature that is essential to Scandinavian style, pulling the whole colour scheme together.

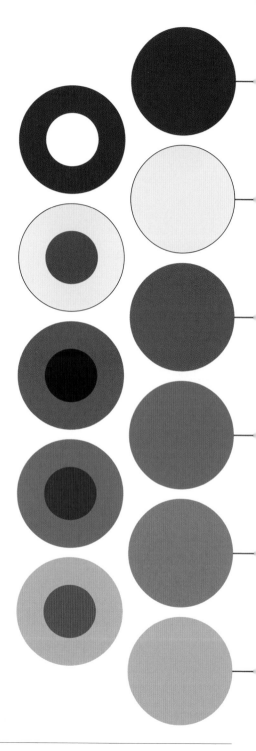

Georg stool

The Georg stool was designed by Chris Liljenberg Halstrøm in 2013. It is an adaptable piece that is useful in the bedroom because it can be used as a seat or, without the cushion, as a bedside table. The pale wood and simple yet elegant design reflect Scandinavian style. The stool is part of the Georg collection, which includes a console table (not shown here) that could also be used as a vanity table. The woollen cushion is fitted loosely with a leather string, adding natural materials to your bedroom.

Halstrøm is influenced by her Nordic roots (she has a Swedish mother and Danish father) and was encouraged to draw from a young age. After studying in Stockholm and Berlin, she graduated in 2007 from The Royal Danish Academy of Fine Arts in Copenhagen, which is when she established her own studio.

The Georg collection was part of the official Danish exhibition, Mindcraft, at the Milan Furniture Fair in 2013. The Danish company Skagerak agreed to manufacture, and the stool has proved successful, winning multiple design awards.

Designer
Chris Liljenberg Halstrøm

Manufacturer
Skagerak

Year
2013

Place
Denmark

Material(s)
FSC-certified raw or painted oak; leather strap; wool-blend cushion

Dimensions
Height: 46 cm
Width: 45 cm
Depth: 32 cm

Gräshoppa table lamp

The iconic Gräshoppa lamp was designed by Greta Magnusson-Grossman and first produced in 1947. Already established as a designer in Sweden, in 1940 Greta Magnusson-Grossman emigrated to Los Angeles, where she opened a shop, Magnusson-Grossman Studio on Rodeo Drive. It was a huge hit, and its client list included such names as Greta Garbo, Joan Fontaine and Gracie Allen.

Magnusson-Grossman's simple, compact and functional lamp fits well with Scandinavian style. It has a lithe frame and an elongated conical shade that rotates to direct light where needed, making this a great bedside light for reading.

The Gräshoppa lamp was relatively unknown before Danish manufacturer Gubi started producing a reproduction according to original drawings in 2010. The lightweight, modern and aesthetically appealing lamp quickly rose to iconic status and made it onto the wishlist of all Scandinavian-style lovers.

Designer
Greta Magnusson-Grossman

Manufacturer
Gubi

Year
1947

Place
Denmark

Material(s)
Powder-coated steel shade; solid brass frame and hardware; fabric-covered cord

Dimensions
Height: 41 cm
Width: 14 cm
Depth: 14 cm

Hästens bed

Pehr Adolf Janson (1830–1885) was from the first generation in the Hästens bedding company and is the rightful founder of the brand, but it wasn't until 1978 that the iconic blue-check bed was created by Jack Ryde. In the 1970s, the popular colours were brown, orange and green. When the vibrant blue-checked upholstery was first revealed in Sweden, it was criticized, as the colour was so different from the trends of that time. However, Hästens proved its critics wrong; the bed has gone on to become a style icon and, since the 1970s, has become the Ferrari of beds greatly due to its colour.

The darker blue of this design doesn't exactly scream Scandinavian style, as it is not a colour we see anywhere else, but as a Hästens owner, you don't care. Comfort is key. The fabric is a jacquard weave made of one hundred per cent cotton and uses eco-friendly dyes. The beds are handcrafted using the same natural materials as when they were first developed over 160 years ago. The beds come in various versions; for instance, some have headboards and others are electronically adjustable for sitting up and reading.

Designer
Jack Rhyde

Manufacturer
Hästens

Year
1978

Place
Sweden

Material(s)
Jacquard-weave cotton fabric; double pocket spring system; solid Swedish-oak frame

Dimensions
(Double, pictured)
Height: 69 cm
Width: 210 cm
Length: 220 cm

Våg chest of drawers

The Våg chest of drawers was designed by Nirvan Richter in 2008. This timeless piece is influenced by classic furniture from the mid-century, but its modern good looks come from its elegant lines and use of materials: the curved inset handles, rounded corners and black powder-coated steel base. It can be used to store clothes and to display accessories and artwork.

Nirvan's work reflects Scandinavian style through his use of natural materials, functionality and simplicity. His furniture uses wood that comes from sustainable sources, and it has been eco-labelled by the World Wide Fund for Nature since 1999.

From an early age, Nirvan loved furniture design, in particular the work of some of Scandinavia's great furniture designers, such as Børge Mogensen, Alvar Aalto and Bruno Mathsson. He first showed his furniture at a fair in Karlskrona in Sweden in 1993. Such was his success that he went on to found his own company, Norrgavel.

Designer
Nirvan Richter

Manufacturer
Norrgavel

Year
2008

Place
Sweden

Material(s)
Oak and powder-coated metal

Dimensions
Height: 51 cm
Width: 218 cm
Depth: 38 cm

Kay Bojesen Monkey

The Monkey was designed by Kay Bojesen in 1951. This toy has become a favourite as a gift for young children and can be found in many Scandinavian children's bedrooms. The design is simple, solid and tactile, encouraging children to play and interact with it. The different-coloured wood and moving parts subtly bring out the features of each animal.

The Monkey is part of a family of animals that includes a dog, a bear, an elephant, a hippo and a rabbit created in 1957, a year before Bojesen's death.

In 1908, Kay Bojesen first started working in metal, as an apprentice at the Danish metal and silver company, Georg Jensen. In 1919, he became a father, and it was then that he started to make wooden toys for his children, inspired by those his father had made for him.

In 1990, Bojesen's family gave Rosendahl Design Group the rights to produce, distribute and sell Kay Bojesen's designs under the brand name Kay Bojesen Denmark. They have successfully marketed these iconic animals so that today they are as popular as ever.

Designer
Kay Bojesen

Manufacturer
Rosendahl Design Group

Year
1951

Place
Denmark

Material(s)
Teak and limba wood

Dimensions
Height: 20 cm

Author biography

Allan Torp is a Danish writer and blogger. He has contributed to and been featured in magazines and newspapers worldwide. He has also consulted on new product development and designs for several leading Danish design companies.

Allan runs the international blog Bungalow5.dk, for those who are passionate about design in all its forms, seeking inspiration and unique ways to achieve a modern, comfortable and stylish home. His vision is to create a platform where Scandinavian style can be shared throughout the world.

When he's not travelling the world, Allan lives in Copenhagen, Denmark.

Acknowledgements

Quid Publishing and the author would like to
thank Pernilla Algede of Alvhem and Tomas
Backman of Fantastic Frank for kindly supplying
a number of the images used in this book.

Alvhem (www.alvhem.com) opened its doors
in Gothenburg, Sweden, in 2007. It combines a
passion for real estate and interior design with
a love of history and heritage.

Fantastic Frank (www.fantasticfrank.com) is
a real-estate company based in Berlin, Germany,
and Stockholm, Sweden, with additional branches
opening throughout Europe. It was founded by
Tomas Backman, Mattias Kardell and Sven Wallén,
who wanted to create a company that took
seriously the aesthetics and design of the
properties they represented.

The author also wishes to thank the loving,
engaging and ever-growing followers to his blog,
Bungalow5.dk, and the many great brands and
designers who constantly provide inspiration and
share their designs and stories.

Further resources

Books:

Lars Bolander and Heather Smith MacIsaac, *The Scandinavian Home*. Thames & Hudson, 2010

Lars Dybdahl, *101 Danish Design Icons.* Hatje Cantz, 2016

Dorothea Gundtoft, *New Nordic Design.* Thames & Hudson, 2015

Dorothea Gundtoft, *Real Nordic Living*. Thames & Hudson, 2017

Sonia Lucano, *Interior Inspiration: Scandinavia.* Thames & Hudson, 2016

Monocle, *The Monocle Guide To Cosy Homes.* Gestalten, 2015

Michael Müller (ed.), *Børge Mogensen: Simplicity and Function*. Hatje Cantz, 2017

Christian Holmsted Olesen, *Wegner – Just One Good Chair*. Hatje Cantz, 2016

Meik Wiking, *The Little Book Of Hygge: The Danish Way to Live Well*. Penguin Life, 2016

Blogs:

Stylizimo
www.stylizimo.com

Elisabeth Heier
elisabethheier.no

Only Deco Love
www.onlydecolove.com

September Edit
www.septemberedit.com

My Scandinavian Home
www.myscandinavianhome.com

Ollie & Seb's House
ollieandsebshaus.co.uk

Scandinavia Standard
www.scandinaviastandard.com

A Merry Mishap
www.amerrymishapblog.com

Credits

72: Wing Chair designed by Hans J. Wegner, produced by Carl Hansen & Søn

73: Pelican Chairs at Roll & Hill in New York. Photo: House of Finn Juhl

73: Arsenalsgatan 6A – Pernilla Algede, Alvhem

74–77: The Danish Home Stockholm. Interior Stylist Pella Hedeby. Photographers Evan Pantiel and David Thunander. Manufacturer Erik Jørgensen.

79: Hammarby Allé 53b, photo Anna Malmberg, stylist Linda Palmcrantz

80: Beosound 2, produced by Bang & Olufsen

82: OSLO chair, designed by Anderssen & Voll, produced by Muuto 84: Retreat sofas. Photography by Mathias Nero

86: String shelving. Designed by Nils Strinning, produced by String®

88: POÄNG chair designed by Noboru Nakamura for IKEA

90: Penguin Chair by Ib Kofod Larsen. Photo by Nick Nemechek

95, 96: Kastellgatan 16 – Pernilla Algede, Alvhem

98: Västmannagatan 17, stylist Josefin Hååg

99: BIG – Bjarke Ingels Group kitchen design, image by Reform

99: Line Thit Klein. (Line Klein Studio)

105: Kim Dolva's house (owner of KBHS Nedkeri), designed + furniture made by him, photographed by Gyrithe Lemche

106: Tools casserole, designed by Björn Dahlström for Iittala

108: KH Wurtz ceramics, image kindly supplied by Sigmar London (retailer of KH Wurtz ceramics in the UK)

110: Cylinda Line coffee pot designed by Arne Jacobsen for Stelton

112: Perfection red wine glass, designed by Tom Nybroe for Holmegaard; image supplied by Holmegaard

116: © GAP Interiors/Nick Smith - Interior designer – Leonie Walker 117: Ringvägen, stylist Emma Wallmen, photo Anna Malmberg

119: AAC22 Oak Matt Lacquer chair, designed by Hee Welling and White Loop Stand Round Table, designed by Leif Jørgensen for Hay

120: Cover chair designed by Thomas Bentzen for Muuto; copyright © Finnish Design Shop, 2004–2017

121: Hedåsgatan 20 – Pernilla Algede, Alvhem

122, 124: Södra Vägen 71. Design: The owners. Photo: Cim Ek

127: Seglatsgatan 14, stylist Emma Wallmén, photo Mikael Axelsson

128: Upholstered Beetle Chair designed by GamFratesi, produced by GUBI, GUBI Press photo

130: Blown pendant, designed by Samuel Wilkinsons for &tradition 132: The Essay™ table, designed by Cecilie Manz for Fritz Hansen image fritzhansen.com

136: Vilda 2 chair, designed by Jonas Bohlin in 2012 for Gemla

140: © GAP Interiors/Julien Fernandez – Margaux Beja

142: Blekingegatan 44; stylist Ida Lauga

143: Hoburgsvagen 21, stylist Åsa Copparstad, photo Emma Jonsson Dysell

144, 146: Fjärde Långgatan 10e. Interior design: The owner, Pernilla Algede / House of Beatniks. Photo: Alice Johnsson

149: Majorsgatan 4 – Pernilla Algede, Alvhem

150: HV1 mixer tap by VOLA

152: Vipp pedal bin

154: Over Me by Morten & Jonas for Northern Lighting

156: Framed mirror, designed by Anderssen & Voll, produced by Muuto

158: PRIME free-standing bathtub in matt Solidsurface, image courtesy of Inbani

160–161: © Jodie Johnson | Shutterstock

163: Hvitfeldtsgatan 14 – Pernilla Algede, Alvhem

164: Heleneborgsgatan 5C, stylist Linda Palmcrantz, photo Mikael Axelsson

165: Nordhemsgatan 66 C – Pernilla Algede, Alvhem

166: Werftstrasse 2, stylist Santiago Brotons, photo Joakim Johansson

167: Katerina Dima/Only Deco Love

168,170: Auping

173: Falugatan 19, photo Joakim Johansson, stylist Josefin Hååg

174: Georg Interior design by Chris Liljenberg Halstrøm, producer Skagerak

176: Gräshoppa Task Table Lamp designed by Greta Magnusson-Grossman, produced by GUBI. GUBI Press photo

178: Hästens 2000T/ Hästens

180: Våg chest of drawers, designed by Nirvan Richter for Norrgavel; photographer Pelle Wahlgren for Norrgavel

182: Kay Bojesen Denmark Monkey, image supplied by Kay Bojesen Denmark

Index